# ISLAM AND CHRISTIANITY

# ISLAM AND CHRISTIANITY

*a Muslim and a Christian*
*in Dialogue*

by
Badru D. Kateregga
David W. Shenk

WILLIAM B. EERDMANS PUBLISHING COMPANY
*Grand Rapids, Michigan*

First published 1980 by Uzima Press Ltd., Kenya
Revised edition published 1981
This American edition published 1981 through special
arrangement with Uzima by Wm. B. Eerdmans Publishing Co.,
255 Jefferson Ave. S.E., Grand Rapids, MI 49503

**Library of Congress Cataloging in Publication Data**

Kateregga, Badru D.
Islam and Christianity.

Bibliography: p. 181
1. Islam — Relations — Christianity.    2.  Christianity
and other religions — Islam.    I.  Shenk, David W., 1937-
BP172.K345    1981      230      81-3164
ISBN 0-8028-1891-9      AACR2

# Contents

# Acknowledgements

We wish to express our sincere gratitude to Mr Ali A.A. El-Maawy, Education Officer, Ministry of Basic Education, Kenya, and Director of *Tabliqh* and *Daawa* (Religious Affairs) in the Supreme Council of Kenya Muslims (SUPKEM), for reading the manuscript and making very valuable suggestions. We are also indebted to Sheikh Ali Darani, Qadhi of Mombasa, for reading through some of our chapters and making various comments. We have also to thank Dr Omar Hassan Kasule of Mulago Hospital, Uganda, Sheikh Ahmad Mukasa, Secretary for Religious Affairs in the Uganda Muslim Supreme Council, Sheikh Edrisa Songolo, Deputy Qadhi, Busoga Province, Uganda, Mr. Ismail Gyagenda of Makerere University, Sheikh Burhan Ssebayigga of Islamic Development Bank Jedda, Saudi Arabia and Mr. Atiq Quraishy, Ministry of Higher Education, Kenya, for insight and answering a number of inquiries we put to them.

We further acknowledge our indebtedness to the Right Reverend Dr Kenneth Cragg and Professor William Bijlefeld, who read portions of the manuscript and made valuable suggestions. Others who gave counsel, particularly on the Christian portions of the manuscript, included the Reverend Dr Peter Ipema, former general advisor for the Islam in Africa Project (IAP), and the current advisor, Reverend Dr James P. Dretke. Mr Silas Wanda, who is project officer for the IAP also contributed counsel. Other IAP advisors who read the early versions of the manuscript included Reverend Richard Moller-Petersen, Sierra Leone, Reverend Donald Bobb, Ivory Coast and Reverend Nils Ronnbeck, Kenya. Reverend and Mrs Ron Ward of the African Christian Church and Schools as well as Mr Fred Kniss, Reverend Roy Brubaker, Mrs Bertha Beachy, and Reverend Paul Zehr of the Mennonite Church were most helpful. Reverend Isaiah Muita of World Vision International also assisted.

We are especially indebted to our wives, Faridah and Grace, for carefully typing the manuscript, and for their constant encouragement and advice. To the rest of our families, we are grateful for their patience in bearing with us while preparing this work.

viii

The Reverend Horace Etemesi of Uzima Press Limited, Kenya, put in many hours of consultation with us; as our publisher he certainly went beyond the call of duty. Similar appreciation is extended to Mr. Nathan O. Kayonde whose theological perspectives were constructive.

Both Kenyatta University College, Nairobi, Kenya, and the Eastern Mennonite Board, Salunga, Pennsylvania deserve special mention. Both have contributed resources in their respective ways for the completion of this book.

Unless otherwise indicated, all quotations from the English translation of the Qur'an are taken from: *The Meaning of the Glorius Koran,* an explanatory translation by Mohammed Marmaduke Pickthall, George Allen and Unwin Limited, London, 1961.

The Scripture quotations in this publication are from: *The Revised Standard Version* of the Bible, copyright 1946, 1952, © 1971, 1973 by the Division of Christian Education of the National Council of the Churches of Christ in the U.S.A., and used by permission.

BADRU D. KATEREGGA<br>
DAVID W. SHENK

## The Authors' Note on Transliteration

We have deliberately omitted some marks in the transliteration of Arabic words in the interest, we hope, of our readers who are not familiar with Arabic.

B.D.K.<br>
D.W.S.

# Foreword

by Sheikh Abdulla Saleh Farsy,
the Chief Kadhi of Kenya

As a Muslim it would be unreal for me not to be impressed by
the bravery of the two authors to write with honesty, tolerance,
courtesy and extreme politeness on the fundamental matters
of the two religions, expressing the stand of each on matters
of faith in God and Prophethood, the meaning of evil and sin,
etc., without attempting to try to make the reader believe
in the rightness of one faith over the other. Badru Kateregga
and David Shenk could be among the first to attempt such a
dialogue, which lets the reader to be the sole judge of the
message behind the contents. Sheikh Zakariya Razy (not
Rhaze) in one of his books wrote about the different schools
of thought in Islam, stating the merits of each one of them
without prejudice over the other, without suggestion of the
rightness of the convictions, for instance, of the Al-Ash-ariya
over the Qadariya or the Qadariya over the Jabariya and vice-
versa, although he himself belonged to Al-Ash-ariya. His book
was a comparative study of the different schools of thoughts
and sects in Islam. It was received with admiration by all
scholars irrespective of their convictions. Badru Kateregga and
David Shenk have gone a step further by undertaking a similar
kind of discussion on the two religions themselves.

This is a worthy attempt between these two scholars who
with good intents in their hearts thought of bringing out in one
volume the creed of the two main religions of the world.
Each in his own faith has stated exactly what his religion stands
for without a compromise, despite their response at the end of
each chapter. Each has conveyed in as straight-forward language as possible the stand of his scriptures. Badru Kateregga
being a lecturer by profession presented the facts as he knew
them from the Quran and the traditions (Sunnah) of the Prophet
Muhammed (peace be upon him) without elaboration or attempt
to convince the reader. David Shenk being a Pastor and a
University lecturer stated his facts in the language of a preacher
which carried somewhat a little attempt to convince yet clearly

restraining from doing so. Besides this slight imbalance in the dialogue, it is hard to read this book and not admire the motive of the two writers to undertake such a task. What was it? Could it have been an academic exercise or a call to present to the reader the religion of God? May be the reader will see it this way—presenting the two religions in front of a faithful Muslim and a faithful Christian for them to compare. Faith is a state of belief which has very strong fixation. Comparison is for something with two comparable facts or sets of alternatives. In the religious faith the principle of comparability or alternating with another faith hardly exists, if it does at all. Where there are similarities, they are always predecessed by conditions and buts. To the Muslim the miraculous birth of Jesus and the Virginity of Mary are part of his faith. God said be and Jesus became.

'Thus God creates whatever He wills. He commands a thing to be and it is' (Quran 3: 46). To the Christian the miracle is not only of the birth, but also of the descent of God into man. The two sets of faiths are incomparable. One is of man and a prophet being decreed by God to be born miraculously, as Adam was created out of nothing, so to speak. The other is of the same person as Son of God, whose extension into a human form was to come through being born by a woman.

The oneness of God which is presented by Badru insists on God being one in His own Oneness. There is neither extension nor incarnation. His coming to men is His omnipresence in them and with them at every time and every place. The Christian Unity of God is in the Trinity; the Three in one. There is no oneness without his extension unto His Son, and the Holy Spirit. His coming to men was in flesh of a human being, in the way of the human life and habits. The Christian believes that the Trinity is always in his presence. This way of belief is all over the book. The principle of original sin does not exist in Islam. Man is born in primordial innocence. Adam was forgiven and cleansed of the sin before his descent to earth, so Badru explained. Sin is never inherited in Islam. Men are judged by their merits.

When we accept this understanding of the uncompromising state of the dialogue of these two authors, then we can appreciate the value of this book. The admirable factors for us all are the tolerance and respect which have been demonstrated in this work, by each writer responding to the other's chapter in politeness and restraint, without arguments or claim for justification.

For those who want to know Islam this book gives them an opportunity to read it in its most fundamental form. For those who want to learn about Christianity the book presents to them in simple language the creeds of Christian faith. It appears to me that the two authors agreed to present to the world two books in one, with a difference that each responded to the witness of the other. Maybe that was their meeting ground, and both being concerned with teaching of comparative religion, that could have been a natural one.

The Prophet Muhammad (peace be upon him) used to debate with Christians in a kind atmosphere. He never showed hardness or severity which characterised his debates with Polytheists (mushrikun) and idol worshippers. He argued on the basis of scriptures as he was told in the Quran, 'God asked Jesus, Son of Mary: "Did you ask the people to take you and your mother as two gods beside God?" Jesus answered: "Praise be to You alone, I had not said but that which I was commanded to say. You surely know whether I am guilty of such blasphemy, for You know all that is in my thoughts and I know none of what is in Yours. You alone are omniscient. I did convey to them that which You commanded me to convey, namely that they ought to worship God alone, my Lord and their Lord. In their midst I have been a witness unto you throughout my life"' (Quran 5:116-118).

Sheikh Abdulla Saleh Farsy

# Foreword

by The Right Reverend Dr. Kenneth Cragg

Was it wise to invite a Foreword to this venture from one so fully committed to its themes and purpose? It might have been well to ask a commendation from a sociologist. He might have withheld it on the ground that the text was so heavily theological and seemed unaware of the sanctions of community and communal consciousness which so largely determine the mental positions we take even when they are irenic. Or perhaps an introductory note from a Marxist who would, no doubt, have remarked how absent was the element of realism about economic structures and their part in religious attitudes. He would certainly have noticed the strong individualism of the concepts of evil especially on the Islamic side, and wondered about the sanguine view implied about the innocence of structures, including those of religion itself.

Or perhaps a preview should have been entrusted to some master of African culture and anthropology to bring the whole more squarely into what President Kenyatta, in a notable pioneer study, called *Facing Mount Kenya.* Such an introducer would have noted how strangely absent from the discussion was the field of symbol and ritual and ancestors. He would probably have queried the ready reliance on conceptual thinking and verbal exposition. He might have wondered whether both authors alike had not been too unsuspectingly western in their approach. But then, he would have said, all dialogue is liable to be that way.

Or perhaps it should have been someone like Bertolt Brecht the German poet and playwright of the forties and fifties, who was once asked what he would suggest for his tombstone and replied: 'Write that I was an uncomfortable person, and that I expect to remain so.' For he had that radical sense which bracingly questioned all religious assurance, yet did so with a wistfulness that made unbelief sensitive and warm. How can we be so sure of authority when God seems so elusive? Have our convictions about revelation really reckoned with how baffling are the experiences of our mortality? Are we honest

enough in our ideal claims about the Ummah 'transcending
ethnic and cultural barriers,' or the Church 'embracing all
mankind.'?   In our doctrines of transcendence—whether what
Badru Kateregga calls 'the absolute legal sovereignty of Allah,'
or David Shenk 'the infinite love of God'—have we adequately
measured the secular perplexities which cannot find their
relevance amid the apparent ultimates of contemporary history.
Have we believers in His presence sufficiently understood the
secular experience of His absence—or His hiddenness?   And,
perhaps most of all, in our assurance about man, whether
Islamic man, perfectible and merely frail, or Christian man,
graced in Christ and redeemable, have we truly realised how
demonic he may be?  Jewish thinking, such as Martin Buber's,
might sober both of us in this regard.

Or perhaps, again, we should ask a poet to do a frontispiece.
Pasternak perhaps, or Walter De La Mare, or Wole Soyinka.  For
poetry has a way of refining the prose of our ideas into the
feel of mystery and so taking the mind into the heart.  Conversation might then be less articulate and serviceable, but also
more intimate and open.   Or perhaps we should request a
Buddhist to do our preface, and bring a quite contrasted
angle of vision to our relationships.

Valuable, and salutary, as any of these alternatives would
be, the authors have not invited them.  Their choice falls on
me, and I am happy to serve.  For I fully share their hopes and
concerns and it is a privilege to commend them to a wide range
of readers both in East Africa and beyond.  But in doing so
I would want to have in mind the queries and misgivings of the
conceivable other choices for this role.  I hope all readers will
have an awareness, too, of how these other perspectives relate
to what they find.

But, given, the pattern the authors have followed, two
impressions emerge.  The first is how far we have come away
from polemic and barren controversy.  To use a phrase of
Peter in his New Testament letter, 'this is thankworthy.'  It is
important that it should deepen and widen among us.  For there
are still sad areas of what might be called 'fanatical consciousness,' which remain quite impervious to love and honesty.
Rejectionism has a way of growing by psychic factors, feeding

upon itself and stiffening its obduracy. We can never be sanguine that we have overcome it: we must always be dedicated to doing so.

The other impression is that consciousness within religious establishments of faith and practice, though free from the fanatical, can still remain unresponsive to meaning from outside. This, in a way, is the frustration of dialogue. As in the present study, we each state our case. We indicate differences. We disentangle misunderstandings. We re-affirm positions. We maintain politeness. We even repent. But what then? For the most part we still stay within our positions, sometimes still failing to take what the other means. Response sometimes reveals that we are not responding. There are numerous examples here. To query God's 'resting on the seventh day' on the ground that He is almighty and needs no rest; to note that it may have been Jibril in 'the burning bush' in comment on the theme of God in history; to disown anthropomorphism in discussion of analogy—all these indicate a non-penetration of meaning. The situation is mutual.

It seems to suggest that we should try, now, to move away from position-statements, with courteous rejoinders, and try, with the continuing courtesy, to develop areas of experience which, while involving what is at issue in the familiar divergencies of view, focus it vitally in terms we both experience and terms which, hopefully, neither of us sponsor as sole proprietors. This may allow us to *escape* from the formalism of dogma and positional thinking and *into* genuine enterprise of of mind and spirit. Perhaps I can put the point by saying that we will then get our bearings by our compass of faith rather than stay believers by a tether of authority.

In confessing transcendence, for example, we might transcend our familiar custodianship and explore the way in which man absolutises his structures in history, even his religious ones, and so commits the *Shirk* of idolatry. Then we may see the theme of unity and *Tauhid* as essential, not propositional, as having to do not with number but with the effective rule of God, relativising all else. In the same context, we might explore sin in the world, as the late Dr. Muhammad Kamil Husain did in Cairo, not in abstract terms about Adam's lapse of rebellion, but in the concrete form of communal pride, pseudo-loyalties and corporate expedience, such as we all experience today.

I suppose it would be right to say that the central controversy between Islam and Christianity has to do with the distancing, or otherwise, between the divine and the human. It is this which pervades all the themes of revelation, prophetic vocation, the ways of divine mercy, the categories of law and love, the degree of *Kenosis* in creation itself on God's part, and the question of Jesus and the Cross. It is urgent for us to live together in the depth of these issues, neither foreclosing them by anathemas, nor obscuring them by neglect. Rather we should let them press the more fully upon us by virtue of our openness to common action in the day to day scene and by our readiness to think second, even third, thoughts about the responses we first instinctively make.

This is, no doubt, a sense of vocation which not all will discover. Many readers of these Chapters will find in them what they seek, namely a quiet re-iteration of what they believe. They will wholeheartedly welcome it by half! It may even serve useful purposes that way. For it is important that we should know where we are and have a careful, respectful statement of our case. Others will wish that the brief rejoinders to the position chapters had been either less predictable or more full.

But the task to which our authors set their hand is continuing business. Their readership will be the clearer for their patience, frankness and sincerity both in approach and exposition. They have presented both the assets and the liabilities of the relationship between their faiths. Africa, by and large, has a better tradition of inter-faith co-existence than other continents. What the African ethos will yet do with the external heritage of church and mosque belongs to the future, but a future steadily being shaped in decisions of the present. Authors like ours will best be rewarded by those they help readers to take, each in his and her own integrity of mind and heart.

Kenneth Cragg

# Preface

Hundreds of millions of Muslims and Christians are neighbours to each other. The faithful in both communities believe that they have been called by God to be witnesses. Yet they seldom hear each other witness. The collision of their histories has created walls which separate. Although both communities worship the same God and seek to be the people of God, they seldom listen to one another

This book is an attempt by a Muslim and a Christian to witness and to listen. We, the authors, are close friends. We have taught together in the Department of Philosophy and Religious Studies at Kenyatta University College, Kenya. Badru Kateregga, a Muslim, taught Islamic history and theology. David Shenk, a Christian, taught Christian history and theology. Both of us have taught comparative religion together in a team-teaching relationship. Often the team-teaching was a dialogue, a witness from one faith to another in the presence of our students.

We have sensed that the dialogue in witness between Muslims and Christians is not a joke. It is exceedingly serious. The issues are profound. They are about the basic questions of the human situation. The seriousness of the issues means that in the hearing and the giving of witness in dialogue there is pain. Perhaps we mutually fear the pain. Perhaps that is one reason Muslims and Christians so seldom speak with one another concerning faith.

Nevertheless, we, the authors, believe that witness in dialogue is vital. We need to learn to speak with one another from within our respective communities of faith. That is what we have tried to do in this book. We have not minced words. We have spoken with candour. We have each attempted to be as faithful as possible to the respective witness to which we each believe God has called us.

The book is divided into two sections. The first part is written by Badru as a Muslim faith witness. The second part is written by David as a Christian faith witness.

Each part consists of twelve chapters. At the end of each chapter, a response is included from the one to whom the witness is being given. That is to say, at the end of each of the twelve chapters of Muslim witness, there is a Christian response, and similarly at the end of each of the twelve chapters of Christian witness, there is a Muslim response. In some cases, there is a further statement of clarification following the response.

We have written as individuals and as friends. We are personally responsible for what we have said, for ultimately faith witness is intensely personal. Nevertheless, we do speak from within particular faith communities. Badru has relied heavily on the Qur'an for his presentation and David has based his writing primarily on the Bible. Badru witnesses from within the Sunni experience. David gives his witness from within the evangelical Protestant experience. Yet both have attempted to be sensitive to the total faith communities from which their respective witnesses emerge.

The theological and practical dimensions of faith explored in this book are not exhaustive, but they are indications of the nature of the encounter between Christians and Muslims. It represents a comparative theology which we hope is free of judgementalism and bias. We have tried to stick to our self-imposed rule: Don't interpret my faith for me!

We believe that this book will provide constructive insights for any Muslims or Christians who want to understand the nature of the two great faith communities of Islam and Christianity. We hope that it can be used as a basis for discussion and dialogue between Christians and Muslims.

We also believe this book would be valuable for students in upper high school, Islamic and Christian theological schools, and as an introductory book for university students.

Muslims are usually uncomfortable with Christians writing concerning Islam. Similarly Christians seldom identify with Muslim interpretations of Christianity. This book, jointly authored by a Muslim and a Christian, has been written under the glaring light of mutual presence. Every word which we have written has been honed by the knowledge that we are working together. Honesty, kindness, and sensitivity have, therefore, been absolutely necessary.

# ISLAM AND CHRISTIANITY

# A Muslim Prayer

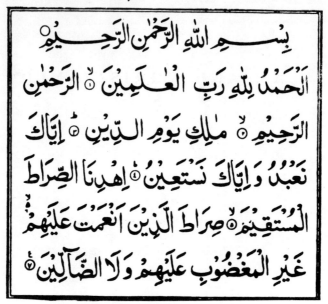

*In the name of God, Most Gracious, Most Merciful.*
*Praise be to God,*
*The Cherisher and Sustainer of the Worlds;*
*Most Gracious, Most Merciful;*
*Master of the Day of Judgement.*
*Thee do we worship,*
*And Thine aid we seek.*
*Show us the straight way,*
*The way of those on whom*
*Thou hast bestowed Thy Grace,*
*Those whose (portion)*
*Is not wrath,*
*And who go not astray.*

(the Fatiha which is the opening chapter
of the Qur'an)

This is the prayer which is repeated by faithful Muslims at least seventeen times a day during the five experiences of corporate prayer.

# A Christian Prayer

Πάτερ ἡμῶν ὁ ἐν τοῖς οὐρανοῖς,
ἁγιασθήτω τὸ ὄνομά σου,
ἐλθέτω ἡ βασιλεία σου,
γενηθήτω τὸ θέλημά σου,
   ὡς ἐν οὐρανῷ καὶ ἐπὶ γῆς.
Τὸν ἄρτον ἡμῶν τὸν ἐπιούσιον δὸς ἡμῖν
   σήμερον·
καὶ ἄφες ἡμῖν τὰ ὀφειλήματα ἡμῶν,
   ὡς καὶ ἡμεῖς ἀφήκαμεν τοῖς ὀφειλέταις
   ἡμῶν·
καὶ μὴ εἰσενέγκῃς ἡμᾶς εἰς πειρασμόν,
   ἀλλὰ ῥῦσαι ἡμᾶς ἀπὸ τοῦ πονηροῦ.

*Our Father Who art in heaven,*
*Hallowed be Thy name.*
*Thy kingdom come,*
*Thy will be done,*
*On earth as it is in heaven.*
*Give us this day our daily bread;*
*And forgive us our debts,*
*As we also have forgiven our debtors;*
*And lead us not into temptation,*
*But deliver us from evil.*

*For Thine is the kingdom and the power*
*and the glory, for ever. Amen.*

   (Matthew 6:9-13)

This is a prayer which Jesus Christ (the Messiah) taught His
disciples to pray, and which is sometimes called the Lord's
Prayer or the Family Prayer.

# PART I  THE MUSLIM WITNESS

*In the Name of Allah, the Compassionate, the Merciful.*

# 1. There is no god but Allah

## THE MUSLIM WITNESS

Islam means total submission to the commands and will of Allah*,
Who is the only true God. The first and greatest teaching of Islam
is proclaimed by the *Shahada* (confession): *La ilaha illa 'llah
Muhammadun rasul Allah*. This means: There is no god but Allah,
and Muhammad is the apostle of Allah. It is this very confession,
which once uttered sincerely and followed completely, makes one
a real Muslim. It is this *Shahada* which leads a Muslim throughout
his life.

Islam is a strictly monotheistic religion. The key *Surah* (chapter)
in the Qur'an testifies to Islam's monotheism.
Say: He is Allah, the One!
Allah, the eternally Besought of all!
He begetteth not nor was begotten.
And there is none comparable unto Him (Qur'an 112).

A Muslim must believe in one God (Allah). Belief in Allah is
the very basis of the *al-Din* (religion) of Islam. Allah Himself has
commanded: 'And cry not unto any other god along with Allah.
There is no god save Him' (Qur'an 28:88). Elsewhere we read:
'Surely pure religion is for Allah only' (Qur'an 39:3).

## God is One

No human language is good enough to describe God, for there is
nothing else like Him. God's nature is far beyond our limited
conception. Nevertheless, we do know that He is one. Allah, the

---

*The word Allah is Arabic and is difficult to translate exactly. The word means
the unique God Who possesses all the attributes of perfection and beauty in
their infinitude. Muslims feel strongly that the English word 'God' does not
convey the real meaning of the word 'Allah'. However, in this book 'Allah' and
'God' will be used interchangeably.

one true God, is not far from us, for He is with us always. The Qur'an says: 'We (God) are nearer to him (man) than his jugular vein' (Qur'an 50:16).

Allah is one, and only He is God. He is the only one worthy of worship. Allah said, 'Choose not two gods. There is only One God. So of Me, Me only, be in awe' (Qur'an 16:51).

All other things and beings which man both knows and knows not are God's creatures and we must recognize that all forms of God's creation are not in any way to be compared to Him. 'I am only a warner, and there is no God save Allah, the One, the Absolute' (Qur'an 38:66).

In another verse God says: 'Follow that which is sent down unto you from your Lord, and follow no protecting friends beside Him' (Qur'an 7:3).

So, because God is one, no one else can share even an atom of His Divine power and authority. God alone possesses the attributes of Divinity. Because God is one and one only, to associate any being with God is both a sinful and an infidel act.

Islam makes it clear that God has no son, no father, no brother, no wife, no sister and no daughters. The pre-Islamic (*jahiliyya*) idea, of calling goddesses (al-Manat, al-Lat, al-Uzza) daughters of Allah, was condemned by the Prophet (peace be upon him) for Allah has no need for daughters. In His unity, God is not like any other person or thing that can come to anyone's mind. His qualities and nature are conspiciously unique. (He has no associates.)

### God the Creator

A Muslim must believe that Allah is the Creator of the universe and everything in it. The Qur'an says: 'He it is Who created the heavens and the earth in truth' (Qur'an 6:73). It adds,

Lo! your Lord is Allah Who created the heavens and the earth in six days, then mounted He the Throne. He covereth the night with the day, which is in haste to follow it, and hath made the sun and the moon and the stars subservient by His command. His verily is all creation and commandment. Blessed be Allah, the Lord of the Worlds (Qur'an 7:54).

These verses remind us that nothing can come to life on its own. Everything, including the earth we live on and the heavens we see above, was created by the Almighty God.

God does not merely create and abandon His creatures. He

goes on fashioning and evolving new forms, and sustaining all that He has created according to His ways. 'He is Allah, the Creator, the Shaper out of naughts, the Fashioner. His are the most beautiful names' (Qur'an 59:24). He is the Sustainer of the universe.

God has created man and kindly provided for him. Concerning the creation of man the Qur'an says:

> He it is Who created you from dust, then from a drop (of seed) then from a clot, then bringeth you forth as a child, then (ordaineth) that ye attain full strength and afterward that ye become old men—though some among you die before—and that ye reach an appointed term, that haply ye may understand (Qur'an 40:67, 68).

God created all that we can see and cannot see, by the Divine command, 'Be', and 'there it was'. By this very command the Lord created the universe and all that is in it.

It is the sincere Muslim belief that God did not rest after creating the universe and all the creatures. He needs no rest like man and animals. God is absolute life, which is free from any such need. The Qur'an says:

> There is no God save Him, the Alive, the Eternal. Neither slumber nor sleep overtaketh Him. Unto Him belongeth whatsoever is in the heavens and whatsoever is in the earth (Qur'an 2:255).

God is active as the Creator, the Life Giver and Life Remover, the Sustainer and the sole Controller of all His creation.

## The names of God

God is the Supreme Reality. He has revealed to mankind ninety-nine beautiful names (*al-asma al husna*) which indicate His transcendent majesty and unity. The Qur'an says: 'Allah's are the fairest names. Invoke Him by them. And leave the company of those who blaspheme His names. They will be requited what they do' (Qur'an 7:180).

In a *Hadith** reported by Abu Huraira, the Prophet (PBUH) is reported to have said: 'Verily there are ninety-nine names of Allah, and whosoever recites them shall enter Paradise.'**

---

**Hadith* means Prophetic tradition.

***Reported by Abu Huraira, *Sahih Muslim* Vol. IV, Lahore M. Ashraf-by Siddiqi, 1975, p. 1409.

These names are not used to divide Allah, for Allah cannot be more than one, but rather to express some of His attributes. Muslims use these names in reverence for God, and as part of praise and prayer. God may always be invoked by a name relevant to the need of His beseecher. We shall be describing some of these names, such as *Rahman* (most Gracious), *Rahim* (most Merciful), or *al-Jalil* (most Majestic).

## God is merciful

All *surahs* of the Qur'an except one* begin with the *Basmalah*,** i.e. the statement: 'In the Name of Allah, the Compassionate (or Beneficient), the Merciful'. The *Basmalah* is the common statement a Muslim must recite before doing anything. It constantly reminds the believer of the mercy of God to all His creation. A careful look at the Qur'an shows that there are numerous *ayat* (verses) which describe God's love and mercy for mankind.

Allah says in the Holy Qur'an:

Allah it is Who hath appointed for you night that ye may rest therein, and day for seeing. Lo! Allah is a Lord of bounty for mankind, yet most of mankind give not thanks (Qur'an 40:61).

God continues in another verse:

Allah it is Who appointed for you the earth for a dwelling-place and the sky for a canopy, and fashioned you and perfected your shapes, and hath provided you with good things. Such is Allah, your Lord. Then blessed be Allah, the Lord of the Worlds (Qur'an 40:64).

Man enjoys the mercy of God Who is kind and good. God's mercy is to anyone, believer or unbeliever, obedient or disobedient, Muslim or non-Muslim, black or white.

The Qur'an states:

Allah is He Who created the heavens and the earth, and causeth water to descend from the sky, thereby producing fruits as food for you (Qur'an 14:32).

And He giveth you of all ye ask of Him, and if ye would count the bounty of Allah he cannot reckon it. Lo! man is verily a wrong-doer, an ingrate (Qur'an 14:34).

---

*Surat Tauba (chapter 9).
**In Arabic transliteration the *Basmalah* reads: *Bis-mi-llahi ar-Rahmani ar-Rahim.*

Allah's Mercy = God's Common Grace upon all men

God's mercy for His creation is immeasurable. We cannot
imagine or count His favours to mankind. He gives man food,
drink, the means of movement, and all the necessities of life. He
provides for him irrespective of his behaviour. God has created
man in the best form of creation and has given him everything
he needs for his spiritual and physical growth. He has given all
this to man because of His mercy. God is the all-Merciful, and
through His mercy man attains peace, tranquility, hope, and
confidence. The mercy of God is real and active; it pervades all
the dimensions of the human experience.

Furthermore, God has promised to extend His love to those
who obey His will. His mercy is extended to all mankind; His
love is extended to those who submit to His will. The Qur'an says:
'Say, (O Muhammad, to mankind): If ye love Allah, follow me;
Allah will love you and forgive you your sins. Allah is Forgiving,
Merciful' (Qur'an 3:31).

## God is all-powerful = Absolute Sovereignty

Having seen that God is Compassionate and Merciful, we must
also note that it is only God Who is the possessor of all power.
There is none besides Allah Who can benefit or harm a Person.
Only God can provide for man's needs or give and take away life.
The Holy Qur'an proclaims: 'Knowest thou not that it is Allah
unto Whom belongeth the sovereignty of the heavens and earth;
and ye have not, beside Allah, any friend or helper' (Qur'an 2:107).
With God alone rests the authority to exercise power in the
heavens, on earth, and over the entire creation.

God's supreme authority and power cannot be challenged by
anyone or anything. He is the Supreme Master of the whole
universe as well as its Creator. A Qur'anic verse which comments
on God's sovereign power reads:

Say: O Allah! Owner of Sovereignty! Thou givest sovereignty
unto whom Thou wilt, and Thou withdrawest sovereignty
from whom Thou wilt. Thou exaltest whom Thou wilt and
Thou abasest whom Thou wilt. In Thy hand is the good. Lo!
Thou art Able to do all things (Qur'an 3:26).

This is a serious admonition from Allah to those who hold power
on earth. They should remember that God gives power, and also
removes rulers from power as He pleases. He is capable of doing
this because all power comes from Him; He is the Lord of power.

'Now Allah be exalted, the True King! There is no God save
Him, the Lord of the Throne of Grace. He who crieth unto any

other god along with Allah hath no proof thereof' (Qur'an
23:116–117). This verse explains the nature of the power of God.
He is the most exalted Power, the Sovereign, the Master. The
firm belief in the all-powerful nature of God can help man to
give the best possible explanation of many mysterious things that
happen in life.

Allah is the undisputed Authority Who alone is entitled to
receive obedience, and in fact receives it. He is the most Supreme,
so heads should bow to Him in submission and adoration. Powerful
as He is, God remains pure and free from all sins and evil.

## God is wise and all-knowing

The Omnipotent, Merciful, Benevolent Allah is also all-wise and
all-knowing (omniscient). The Holy Qur'an teaches:

> And keep your opinion secret or proclaim it, lo! He is Knower
> of all that is in the breasts (of men). Should He not know what
> He created? And He is the Subtle, the Aware (Qur'an
> 67:13–14).

Muslims take these attributes of God's knowledge very seriously.
For instance one should not commit sins in the dark thinking that
because there is no one around one is not being noticed. God's
knowledge extends to everything seen and unseen, spoken or
unspoken. Nothing is hidden from Him, desires or undeclared
intentions.

God's wisdom and knowledge is stressed in several verses of
the Qur'an. For instance He says:

> His is the praise in the Hereafter, and He is the Wise, the
> Aware. . . . Not an atom's weight, or less than that or
> greater escapeth Him in the heavens or in the earth, but it
> is a clear record (Qur'an 34:1, 3).

> And He knoweth what is in the land and the sea. Not a
> leaf falleth but He knoweth it, not a grain amid the dark-
> ness of the earth, naught of wet or dry but [is is noted] in a
> clear record (Qur'an 6:59).

It is the perfect God Who knows everything happening in the
present and in the future. He knows what is near and far, what is
in heaven and on earth. His knowledge is unbound. He instructs
man in wisdom through His messengers and written Scriptures.
He also reveals to man the knowlege of the laws of nature and His
wonderful signs in His creation and in the order of the universe.
This is all part of His wisdom and knowledge.

## God is eternal

As Muslims we are strongly commanded to believe and know that God is eternal. By this we acknowledge that God has no beginning and no end, that He has been there and will be there always. There is none after Him nor before Him. He was when there was nothing, and will be when there will be nothing. The Qur'an states: 'He is the First and the Last, and the Outward and the Inward; and He is Knower of all things' (Qur'an 57:3).

The eternal God is not limited by time, space, place, or circumstance. As He exists beyond time, He cannot go into senility. God is pre-existent and eternal, yet other forms of existence will come to an end. Everything that exists will perish except God Who will endure forever. The Qur'an teaches: 'Everyone that is thereon will pass away; There remaineth but the countenance of thy Lord of Might and Glory' (Qur'an 55:26–27). This teaching is important because it reminds the believers that as human beings we are nothing but visitors on this world, that God alone is eternally living and present, and that all else is transient.

The most magnificent works of man like space-craft or sky-scrapers are but nothing in the eyes of God. The great empires, the marvellous works of science, art, and all other spheres of human endeavour will perish. The great wonders of nature such as the mountains, the valleys, the seas, the stars, the sun, the moon will equally perish at the time God wills. Only He, the Supreme Master of the whole universe, and the Creator of everything will remain.

In attempting to understand the nature and works of God, we learn that: God is only One without a partner or son. He is the Creator of the universe and everything that is to be found in the universe. He is the Compassionate and Merciful and His mercy is to all creatures. He is just. He is the Guide and Guardian of everything. He is pre-existent and eternal. He is all-knowing and all-wise. He is loving and provident, and His mercy for His creatures knows no boundary. He is all-powerful and the Supreme Master of all the worlds. He is holy and cannot commit sins or do evil. He is independent and unique.

Because He is unique, man cannot know everything about God, and even the list of ninety-nine names of God is not in any way exhaustive. Nevertheless, the Muslim can acknowledge God through reflection, meditation, firm commitment to the credal

statement, *'La ilaha illa 'llah,* and the total peaceful surrender
to His commands and will.


## A CHRISTIAN RESPONSE

Christians and Muslims worship the same God. Both give witness
that there is one true and only God, Who is the righteous and
transcendent Creator of all things in heaven and earth. Furthermore, Christians accept with thankfulness all the ninety-nine
names of God, which Muslims repeat in worship and praise to
God. Even the name Allah is affirmed by Christians as one of
the names of God. The Prophet Abraham knew God as El or
Elohim, which is a Hebrew form of the Arabic 'Allah'. It is no
wonder that the Qur'an affirms that those closest to the Muslims
are the Christians. The profound Muslim appreciation of the
sovereignty and transcendence of God is a witness which Christians
need to hear.

Nevertheless, within our common faith in God, Muslims and
Christians experience differences. These differences are rooted
in different understandings of God's relationship to man. The
Qur'an stresses the revelation of God's commands and His names
to man. In the Bible we perceive God as the One Who reveals
Himself to mankind.

The Biblical witness is that God has chosen to reveal Himself
in personal self-disclosure with mankind. God as the One Who
encounters personally is known as Yahweh, the covenant God,
the 'I AM', Who is always present calling man into a covenant
relationship with Himself. Yahweh reveals not only His will,
commands, and names to mankind, but also Himself in personal
self disclosure.

The Bible reveals that Yahweh in His self-disclosure reveals
that He is the One Who loves us perfectly. In fact, the Biblical
witness is that Yahweh God gives Himself in suffering, redemptive
love. Because of His love, He sorrows when we sorrow, He suffers
when we suffer, He is pained by our sin. God loves us totally.

The Christian witness is that God invites us into a covenant
fellowship with Himself; God invites us to know and have fellowship with the One Whom Islam praises through the reverent
repetition of His ninety-nine glorious names.

*In the Name of Allah, the Compassionate, the Merciful.*


# 2. The Creation

## THE MUSLIM VIEW

'Lo! your Lord is Allah Who created the heavens and the earth in
six days*' (Qur'an 7:54). The Holy Qur'an and the Traditions
(*Hadith*) of the Holy Prophet (PBUH) describe the Muslim
attitude of praise to Allah for the marvel of creation.

We have already explained in the earlier chapter how God is
the creator of the universe, and all living and non-living things
to be found therein. Our major concern in this chapter will be
to examine the relationship between man, nature, and God,
the Creator of all.

The earth and universe were created by God through a long
step-by-step process. The Qur'an describes the basic process of
the formation of the universe in this way:

> Have not those who disbelieve known that the heavens and
> the earth were of one piece, then We parted them, and We
> made every living thing of water? Will they not then be-
> lieve? And We have placed in the earth firm hills lest it
> quake with them, and We have placed therein ravines as
> roads that haply they may find their way. And we have made
> the sky a roof withheld (from them). Yet they turn away from
> its portents. And He it is Who created the night and the day,
> and the sun and the moon. They float, each in an orbit
> (Qur'an 21:30–33).

These three verses of the Qur'an indicate the evolution of the
ordered world. The Qur'anic witness further testifies that God
created the heavens and earth and what is between them in six
'periods', and no weariness touched Him (Qur'an 50:38). God
created the universe and the earth in an orderly step-by-step

---

*Muslim commentators on the Qur'an feel the six days represent a metaphorical
period. A day in the sight of God can range from 1000 to 50,000 years of our
reckoning (see Qur'an 70:4). These days of creation are in fact long periods
numbering six.

progression. We also learn that all life began in water, a view which is complemented by modern science. The Qur'an further testifies to Allah's ordering the earth:

And He made dark the night thereof, and He brought forth the morn thereof. And after that He spread the earth. And produced therefrom the water thereof and the pasture thereof, And He made fast the hills, A provision for you and for your cattle (Qur'an 79:29–33).

We can deduce from the Qur'anic witness that not only is God the Creator of the whole universe, but that He has also created it in an orderly and understandable manner. Probably man is the last in God's creation process. God has created things in the heavens*, things on earth, things between the heavens and the earth, and things beneath the soil. 'Unto Him belongeth whatsoever is in the heavens and whatsoever is in the earth, and whatsoever is between them, and whatsoever is beneath the sod' (Quran 20:6).

In summary, the Qur'anic witness on creation is as follows: First, there were six periods for the creation in general. Second, there was an interlocking of the stages in the creation of the heavens and the earth. Third, the universe was initially a unique mass all in one block, which God by His power and will split up. Fourth, there is a plurality of heavens and earth, seven heavens being emphasized. Fifth, there is an intermediary world of planets and heavenly bodies between the heavens and the earth. Sixth, God alone is the Creator of nature and the universe, and neither of the two can be God or worshipped as such, for God is altogether transcendent over creation. Seventh, and finally, God created everything in an orderly and understandable manner.

**Man as Khalifa**

It is appropriate to ask ourselves, what role God has given man as far as His creation is concerned? We have already said that man was part of creation, and possibly the last being whom God created. Man was created in a special way. The Lord of the universe bestowed upon man the faculties of learning, speaking, understanding, and discerning the right from the wrong and good from evil. Since man alone possesses these qualities, he enjoys a specially high status in the hierarchy of all known creatures, both in heaven and on earth.

---

*Muslims believe God has created seven heavens: 'Allah it is Who hath created seven heavens, . . .' (Quran 65:12).

The first man God created was Adam. He was the first human being to appear either in heaven or on earth. Adam was created as a *khalifa* (vicegerent) of God on earth. According to the Holy Qur'an, the Lord said to the angels:

> And when thy Lord said unto the angels: Lo! I am about to place a viceroy in the earth, they said: Wilt Thou place therein one who will do harm therein and will shed blood, while we, hymn Thy praise and sanctify Thee? He said: Surely I know that which ye know not (Qur'an 2:30).

After this God created Adam from clay and he was taught the names of all things and the knowledge of their properties (Qur'an 2:31). God then set these things before the angels and asked them, 'Inform me of the names of these, if ye are truthful' (Qur'an 2:31).

Although Adam had been taught the names of all things in the presence of the angels, they could not recall a single name so they replied, 'Be glorified! We have no knowledge saving that which Thou hast taught us. Lo! Thou, only Thou, art the Knower, the Wise' (Qur'an 2:32).

Then God asked Adam to tell the angels all the names of the things taught to him. Adam related correctly all the names as taught much to the surprise of the angels. So God declared the knowledge of His *khalifa* on earth as superior to that of His angels. He ordered all His angels to bow down to Adam; all obeyed except *Iblis* (Satan) who proudly refused and hence rejected the faith. (See Qur'an 2:34).

About this time God created a mate (wife) for Adam to give him company. Her name was Hauwa (Eve). The Qur'an states:

> And We said: O Adam! Dwell thou and thy wife in the Garden, and eat ye freely (of the fruits) thereof where ye will; but come not nigh this tree lest ye become wrongdoers (Qur'an 2:35).

We have observed that Allah created man in a special way, and gave him a special status. Man was to be the *khalifa* of God. Then God taught man the names of all creatures, which he learnt perfectly. He then asked the angels to prostrate to man, which they did except for Satan.* What does all this mean? It means that God gave man the possibility of having control over all things, for to possess the name of a thing would mean to exercise power

---

*Muslim theology is of the view that *Iblis* (satan) was not an angel but a *jinn* (spirit) and that he was a leader of a group of jinns who disobeyed Allah.

over it. The Qur'an says: 'Lo! the earth is Allah's. He giveth it for an inheritance to whom He will' (Qur'an 7:128).

God has honoured man, His *khalifa*, with the authority over His countless creatures. He has been commissioned to use nature for his own welfare (Qur'an 33:72). As a *khalifa*, he is chosen to cultivate the land and enrich life with knowledge and meaning. Nature is subject to man. The superior position held by man in the eyes of God makes man an authority over all God's creation. Man alone enjoys the right to use nature for his own good in obedience to the Divine commands.

The Qur'an teaches:

Allah it is Who hath made the sea of service unto you that the ships may run thereon by His command, ... And hath made of service unto you whatsoever is in the heavens and whatsoever is in the earth (Qur'an 45:12–13).

The sea mentioned here is but one example of Allah's wonderful care in making all things in nature available for the service of man. While subduing nature for his own good, man should remember that it is all from God, and he is only God's *khalifa* on earth. He should, therefore, use nature responsibly in obedience to the revealed commands of God.

**The rights of nature**

Although the superior position of man gives him authority over God's creation, he sometimes oversteps his limits. Islam teaches that all creation has certain rights upon man. This means that man is not free to misuse nature. The fundamental right of God's creation (nature) is that it should not be wasted on fruitless ventures, nor should it be unnecessarily hurt, harmed, or destroyed. For instance, Islam disapproves of the useless cutting of trees and bushes. The *khalifa* can use the fruits and other produce of the forests or grasslands, but has no right to wantonly destroy them. After all, plants and vegetables have got life. 'And We send down from the sky blessed water whereby We give growth unto gardens and the grain of crops,... Provision (made) for men' (Qur'an 50:9–11).

The *khalifa* is free to explore the planets above the earth, but he has no right to attempt destroying them. Islam prohibits the waste of even lifeless things. It even disapproves of the wasteful flow of water; it recommends only a limited and prescribed quantity which one should use for *wudu* (ablution) and *ghusul* (a complete bath).

Even for food, Allah does not permit wastage or excess. It is wrong to overeat when others are hungry. Muslims are allowed to slaughter animals for food, but have been prohibited from killing them for fun, sport, or naughtiness. And when an animal is slaughtered, it should be done with the least possible degree of pain. The name of the Life Giver is besought before slaughter, as a reminder that life must not be taken away thoughtlessly but rather for the purpose of food. Hunting is allowed only if it is for food. However, dangerous and venomous animals may be killed because human life is more precious than that of dangerous animals. Again, they should be killed with the least possible degree of pain. Beasts of burden must be treated kindly and humanely. Birds should not be caged unless there is a very good reason for doing so.

In summary, we have seen that God, the Creator of all, has taught man to use nature, but to avoid the waste and destruction of nature in every way. Nature is the provision of the merciful Allah for the sustenance of man, and man is therefore commanded to make the best use of God's created resources on earth. Responsible stewardship in obedience to God's Divine commands is the key to the Muslim approach to development.

## A CHRISTIAN RESPONSE

Islam and Christianity both recognize that nature is a wonderful creation of God. Man is called by God to use nature with thankfulness and responsibility. The destruction and selfish exploitation of nature is condemned by both Christians and Muslims. Christians identify deeply with the Muslim appreciation of nature as God's good and wonderful creation. They both also recognize their dependence on God in using nature responsibly.

Nevertheless, there seem to be some differences also between the Muslim and Christian understanding of nature. For example, in Islam we learn that God taught man the names of all things; in the Biblical account we read that man was commanded to name the animals. In Islam man is the *khalifa* of God on earth; in Christianity he is commanded to have dominion over the earth. Does this suggest that in the Biblical account man is given considerable personal freedom, authority, and responsibility to use nature for his own good?

However, the Bible does warn that man lives most joyously in his relationships to nature when he is also living in a right and joyous relationship with God.

The purpose of the Bible is to reveal the meaning of life; it is not a book of scientific information. Part of Biblical revelation shows that the earth is God's good and orderly creation. Beyond that the Bible does not go. It is man's own responsibility to understand how God put the earth together, to probe the mysteries of the laws of nature. In the Bible we read that God commanded man to 'subdue', 'fill', 'till', 'rule', 'take care of' the earth.

*In the Name of Allah, the Compassionate, the Merciful.*


# 3. Adam and Hauwa

## THE MUSLIM BELIEF

'I have made him and have breathed into him of My spirit' (Qur'an 15:29). In another Qur'anic verse Allah says: 'Thy Lord said unto the angels: Lo! I am about to place a (*khalifa*) in the earth' (Qur'an 2:30). Muslim scholars are not fully agreed what the meaning is of man as the *khalifa* (vicegerent) of God, or of receiving the spirit of God. Some modern Muslim scholars believe that the Qur'anic evidence suggests that man has a certain God-likeness. But the orthodox belief is that man has no God-likeness. God breathing into man His (God's) spirit is explained by some scholars as the faculty of God-like knowledge and will, which if rightly used gives man superiority over all creation. However, this is not to make God into man, for God is absolutely transcendent.

*[margin note: Not in God's image]*

Nevertheless, man is a dignified, honourable being who has been infused with God's spirit, and has been commissioned to be His *khalifa* on earth. Man enjoys the office of *khalifa*, because he alone of all God's creatures is gifted with the rational faculties, spiritual aspirations, and the powers of conscious action. The Lord of the universe and its Master has created the earth, and has entrusted man to be the caretaker. Allah has granted man a limited autonomy, appointed him as His *khalifa* on earth, and has firmly instructed him to live according to His guidance.

As God has breathed into man His spirit there is, therefore, something in man which is special, something that man was at least bound to retain in some proportion. That special 'thing' is:

(a) The intelligence (or knowledge) to discern between right and wrong, good and evil, real and illusory.
(b) The will to choose freely between good and bad, true and false, right and evil.
(c) The authority to acquire and make use of things around him.
(d) The power of speech—to be able to express his worship of his Creator.

All the above are spiritual qualities which God has entrusted to man, and if rightly used enable man to submit to the will of Allah. We further note that when God created man, He instructed man to worship Him, and none else. He placed man on earth for a fixed time as a test of the manner in which man would use the special spiritual qualities which God has given. God created man to worship Him, and not to be His equal or rival in any way. So, the spiritual qualities of man are proportionate to his finite nature.

Good as man may be, he still cannot measure up to the goodness and perfection of Allah, his Creator. History has shown that man is negligent, careless, and forgetful. He is good, but imperfect. Being imperfect, he needs constant reminding. That is why God sent His prophets and messengers to help man achieve perfection. Through the prophets, God has repeatedly reminded man of the Law of God.

## The first Muslims

It is the Muslim witness that Adam, Allah's first *khalifa* on earth and the first man in creation, was also the first prophet sent for the guidance of mankind. Prophecy begins with the first man. The first man on earth is given clear guidance and a law to follow, and to pass on to his descendents. This law was, and still is, 'Islam'— submission to Allah.

It is the sincere Muslim witness that the first phase of life on earth did not begin in sin and rebellion against the Creator. Although Adam and Hauwa (Eve) were sent from the Heavenly Garden down to earth after Satan's temptation\*, they realized their sin and repented. They sought forgiveness from God. They were given the necessary guidance. Adam was a true Prophet of Allah. They were the first true Muslims.

This is clearly revealed in the Qur'an. We read:

They said: Our Lord! We have wronged ourselves. If Thou forgive us not and have not mercy on us, surely we are of the lost (Qur'an 7:23).

The merciful Allah sent them down to earth with the words:

And We said: Fall down, one of you a foe unto the other! There shall be for you on earth a habitation and provision for

---

\*Satan was also expelled from heaven.

a time (Qur'an 2:36).

Nevertheless man's presence on earth is not a punishment, but rather a test of his commitment to the will of Allah. Although He sent them to earth after Satan's temptation, He certainly forgave them. The Qur'an says: 'Then Adam received from his Lord words (of salvation), and He relented toward him. Lo! He is the Relenting, the Merciful' (Qur'an 2:37).

Because God is all-loving and all-merciful, in spite of man's mistakes, God assured him of guidance. He said: 'Go down, all of you, from hence; but verily there cometh unto you from Me a guidance; and whosofolloweth My guidance, there shall no fear come upon them neither shall they grieve (Qur'an 2:38).

So the first man was given both inspiration and guidance for the whole of mankind. God assures man that anybody who follows this guidance will be free from any fear for the present or the future and any grief for the past.

Many Muslims think that Adam and Hauwa were first kept in the Heavenly Garden for a trial of their inclinations before they were to be sent to the earth where they had been appointed as *khalifa**. The Garden was the most suitable place for the test because it was actually Paradise (*Janna*). Man was shown that Paradise was the suitable place for him to live, but if he yielded to Satan's temptations he could not remain in Paradise. The only way to regain the 'Garden' was to oppose Satan relentlessly and successfully by obeying the Law of God. The Prophet Adam received true guidance so that he himself and his family and descendents could submit to Allah's will as obedient Muslims, and thereby regain Paradise.

It is significant that Hauwa (Eve) was just as responsible for yielding to Satan as was Adam. They were both tempted, they both repented, and were both blessed and forgiven by the merciful Allah. Both were true Muslims. So both woman and man are equal in the sight of God. They are both God's *khalifa* on earth. No Muslim should attribute the first mistake to the woman. In Islam woman is not inferior to man, nor man inferior to woman.

## The frailty of humanity

All people are born as true Muslims, innocent, pure, and free

---

*A. Maududi, *The Meaning of the Qur'an*, Vol. I, Lahore, Islamic Publications Ltd., 1971, pp.58–59.

✳ In Islam, to attribute to woman the 1st transgression is to make her inferior to man.

(Qur'an 30:30). There is no single act which has warped the human will. Any concept of original sin is very much contrary to the true teachings of Islam. It is not a sin for man to be imperfect and fallible. As a finite creature he is bound to be imperfect. However, it becomes a sin if man has the ways and means of *2.* (perfection) and decides not to avail himself of them. Man is not responsible for committing any childhood sin. He only becomes responsible after he grows up, is given intellect by God, and is able to distinguish between right and wrong. This is the only time when he can bear responsibility for his actions before his Creator. Nevertheless, because man is born good, what he becomes after birth is largely the result of external influence and environment.

Although man is a good and responsible being, commiting sinful acts is the responsibility of the actual offender. According to Muslim witness, sin is not hereditary, for no man is born a sinner. Similarly sin is not communal in nature, nor is it transferrable. God has given man freedom of will, and man is therefore personally responsible for his own actions, good or bad, right or wrong. A man can misuse his freedom and fall into corruption and all other vices, but at the same time he is capable of reform and forgiveness if he sincerely chooses to submit to God's guidance. Sin is acquirable, but not innate, and therefore, if man rightly uses those special qualities which he has been endowed with, he can easily avoid sin. Sin is not inevitable, because man is not sinful.

In conclusion, the Muslim view of man can be summarized thus: Man is a dignified, honourable creature, into whom God has breathed his spirit. This spirit can be referred to as God-like knowledge and will; it does not suggest that man is the likeness of God, the equal of God, or the rival of God. The spiritual qualities man has received are only proportionate to his finite nature. Man has also been made God's *khalifa* on earth.

Islam does not believe that humanity is sinful. Rather Islam teaches that man is not perfect. Only God is perfect! But imperfect man forgets and he is negligent. For this reason man has to be reminded constantly of the right path through prophets and revelation.

## A CHRISTIAN RESPONSE

What is man? That is the question. What does it mean for man to receive the 'Spirit of God?' Certainly it does mean that man is the highest creation, just as Islam testifies. The Bible says that man is a little lower than the angels, but crowned with glory and honour (Hebrews 2:7).

The Christian witness enlarges on the Islamic belief that man received the Spirit of God when he was created. The Bible says, 'And the Lord God formed man from the dust of the ground and breathed into his nostrils the breath of life, and man became a living being' (Genesis 2:7). It also says, 'So God created man in His Own image, in the image of God He created him, male and female He created them' (Genesis 1:27). Man created in the image of God does not mean that God looks like man or that man looks like God. But it does mean that man has profound God-like qualities. This God-likeness means especially that man has the capability of fellowship with God. Man can know God. He is capable of enjoying a covenant fellowship with his Creator; he is personal; he is God-like.

Islam emphasizes the intellectual capabilities of man; the Christian faith is especially impressed by man as a covenant or fellowship creature. In Islam man is created for obedience to the will of God. Christians believe that man finds his fullest humanity in joyous communion with God and his fellowman.

The Bible also describes what happens when man turns away from God. When people rebel against God, they become evil and sinful. Christians believe that the image of God in which man was created is spoiled whenever man does not live in a right and joyous relationship with God. The Bible says, 'For all have sinned and fall short of the glory of God' (Romans 3:23).

## A MUSLIM CLARIFICATION

It is doubtful whether the spirit of God which Adam received according to Islam is the same as the Christian understanding of the Spirit of God. As mentioned in the above chapter, Muslims believe that the spirit refers to life which comes from God and which has endowed man with qualities which are superior to other creatures, most notably, superior intelligence, will, authority, and speech.

*In the Name of Allah, the Compassionate, the Merciful.*

# 4. Satan and Evil

## THE SOURCE OF EVIL

It is our sincere belief as Muslims that Satan (*Iblis*) has been at the source and centre of evil even before the creation of Adam, the first human being in history. Satan is the power and source of evil. Satan was the first creature to disobey and lead a rebellion against God, long before the creation of man. The Holy Qur'an relates:

> And (remember) when thy Lord said unto the angels: Lo! I am creating a mortal out of potter's clay of black mud altered, so, when I have made him and have breathed into him of My spirit, do ye fall down, prostrating yourselves unto him. So the angels fell prostrate, all of them together save *Iblis*. He refused to be among the prostrate (Qur'an 15:28-31).*

This disobedience of *Iblis* was the source and origin of evil among mankind. When God asked *Iblis* why he refused to prostrate, he replied: 'Why should I prostrate myself unto a mortal whom Thou hast created out of potter's clay of black mud altered (Qur'an 15:33)? He added that he was far better than man because he was created out of fire (or light). Man was created out of clay.

When God created the first man, infused His spirit into him, appointed him to be His *khalifa*, gave him the names of all things, tested the angels on the same names and they failed, and ordered all the angels to prostrate to Adam, *Iblis* proudly refused, and became an unbeliever; he is, therefore, the source of evil. *Iblis* was very proud that he had been made out of light, and therefore much better than man made out of clay. What *Iblis* had missed was that man, though created out of clay, had been created in the best form, had received part of God's spirit, and had been made a *khalifa* of God. None of these honours had ever been

*See also Qur'an 7:11, 2:34.

bestowed to any other creature, either in heaven or on earth. We see that arrogance, egoism, jealousy, and rebellion, which are the very sources of evil, were (and are) the exclusive possession of Satan.

Because *Iblis* proudly refused to bow down to man, and even abused the angels who prostrated, as well as the man to whom they bowed, God rejected and cursed him. He said: 'Then go thou forth from hence, for verily thou art outcast And lo! the curse shall be upon thee till the Days of Judgement' (Qur'an 15:34–35). Despite the rejection, *Iblis* put in one more request, which was subsequently granted. He said, 'My Lord! Reprieve me till the day when they are raised' (Qur'an 15:36). The reprieve (respite) was granted to *Iblis* until the appointed day. Again the same evil *Iblis* proposed to God thus:

He said: My Lord! Because Thou has sent me astray, I verily shall adorn the path of error for them in the earth, and shall mislead them everyone. Save such of them as are Thy perfectly devoted slaves (Qur'an 15:39–40).

Allah replied to the wicked *Iblis*, who even falsely blamed God for his evil ways:

This is a right course incumbent upon Me: Lo! as for My slaves, thou has not power over any of them save such of the froward as follow thee, and lo! for all such, hell will be the promised place. It hath seven gates, and each gate hath an appointment portion. Lo! those who ward off (evil) are among gardens and watersprings. (And it is said unto them): Enter them in peace, secure (Qur'an 15:41–46).

From this discussion, we learn that *Iblis* has been the arch enemy of man from the time of creation to the present (Qur'an 7:14–18). Satan started his evil activities on the first man whom God had created. He has continued his evil seductions ever since.

After God had cursed *Iblis*, He said to Adam: 'Dwell thou and thy wife in the Garden and eat from whence ye will, but come not nigh this tree lest ye become wrong-doers' (Qur'an 7:19).

At this time our first parents, Adam and Hauwa, were quite innocent in spiritual and material affairs. They had been placed in a spiritual Garden of innocence and bliss which was not on the earth but in the heavens. They did not know evil. However, as God's *khalifa*, they had been endowed, through the spirit of God, with the faculties of knowledge, will, and choice. Although they had the capacity to do wrong, they needed to choose to reject evil.

God, Who is all-knowing, and all-wise, decided to test his *khalifa* by giving him a choice, a small prohibition. In this beautiful 'Garden' man was prohibited from approaching only one tree— the forbidden tree. But he succumbed to the temptations of the Master of Evil.

About this event, the Qur'an says:

> Then Satan whispered to them that he might manifest unto them that which was hidden from them of their shame, and he said: Your Lord forbade you from this tree only lest ye should become angels or become of the immortals. And he swore unto them (saying): Lo! I am a sincere adviser unto you (Qur'an 7:20-21).

So, by deceit, *Iblis* seduced Adam and his wife Hauwa to eat the tree, hence bringing about their fall from the Garden to earth. What was more dramatic is that when they ate, their shame became visible to them for the first time. They hurriedly covered themselves with leaves of the 'Garden'. Soon their Lord called to them saying: 'Did I not forbid you from that tree and tell you: Lo! Satan is an open enemy to you' (Qur'an 7:22)? Thus the chief of evil managed to swerve the progenitors of mankind from the straight path, away from the will of their Lord.

We must also consider that Adam and Hauwa ate the fruit of the forbidden tree as a result of Satan's deceit and temptation. Of course they disobeyed God and thus committed a sin, but at the same time we must realize that actually it was not a wilful and deliberate disobedience. Again we note that when God called on them, they quickly realized their sinfulness, and prayed to Him to forgive them. They did not turn away from God. They said: 'Our Lord! We have wronged ourselves. If thou forgive us not and have not mercy on us, surely we are of the lost' (Qur'an 7:23)!

Adam and Hauwa had felt shame, guilt, and remorse for their disobedience towards Allah. They lost the joyful state of the Garden. That is why they prayed for God's mercy. As Muslims we can deduce from this event that man is imperfect, even if he lives in heaven. At the same time we learn that committing a sin of the gravity of Adam and Hauwa's does not deter the human heart from spiritual reform.

Man as God's *khalifa* has been endowed with sufficient know-ledge to enable him to realize his sins and pitfalls. Better still, this knowledge helps him to know where and to whom to turn for guidance. Islamic witness is that Allah is always ready through

His mercy and grace to forgive the sins of all those who sincerely seek His guidance, and make up their minds to change for the better. The worst sin in Islam is *shirk* (associating Allah with other gods), but even the aetheists, polytheists, or pantheists can be forgiven by Allah if they confess their sins before Allah and sincerely submit to His commands and will.

When Adam and Hauwa prayed for Allah's mercy and forgiveness, they even lacked the correct words of expression, but Allah, Who is all-merciful and most forgiving, taught Adam and Hauwa the prayer for seeking repentance. And Allah pardoned them as the Qur'an witnesses: 'Then Adam received from his Lord words (of revelation), and He relented toward him. Lo! He is the Relenting, the Merciful' (Qur'an 2:37). Adam and Hauwa were thus absolved of the sin of disobedience, and their future descendants were made immune from its effect. Allah did not only accept man's repentance, but went ahead and appointed him as His messenger to give guidance to mankind.

Nevertheless, after Allah had pardoned Adam and Hauwa, He sent them down to earth from the Heavenly Garden. The expulsion from Paradise included *Iblis*, the bitter enemy of man. This is shown in the phrase 'enemies to each other' (Qur'an 7:24), which means that God decreed that *Iblis* and man shall be adversaries of one another. *Iblis* tries his most to divert man from the path of God into the path of evil. But man is commanded, through divine guidance, to fight *Iblis* as his number one enemy. Islam further observes that the evil only touches those who yield to it, and has no power over Allah's sincere servants who have been forgiven because of His mercy.

So, in Islam, evil is avoidable if one is sincere in one's worship of Allah. It is forgivable if the sinner confesses to Allah. It is not hereditary.

The Muslim witness is that *Iblis*, who disobeyed Allah even before the creation of man, is the source of evil. Although the first man Adam and his wife Hauwa sinned, it was not a deliberate desire to disobey their Creator. They were tempted by the master of evil—*Iblis*. They sincerely confessed to Allah, Who granted them pardon. Mankind does not suffer sin and evil because of Adam's disobedience. Sin is not hereditary. Adam having repented was made Allah's first messenger on earth. He was to show guidance to his children. How could God entrust such a high office to an evildoer?

## A CHRISTIAN RESPONSE

The Christian witness is that the origin of evil is the misuse of personal freedom. Satan misused his freedom. He rebelled against God and subsequently became exceedingly evil. Multitudes of angels and spirits have followed his example. The Biblical witness is that Satan tempts man to sin, and man has also decided to yield to Satan's temptation. Adam and Eve chose to disobey God. They took the fruit which God had forbidden. They ran from God and hid in the bushes. They decided to turn away from God (Genesis 3:1-24). The decision of mankind to turn away from God is the root of evil. In our disobedience we become evil. The image of God in which we are created is tragically spoiled because we have collectively and individually turned away from God. God is not to be blamed. We ourselves have turned away from God. For this reason we experience guilt and death. The Biblical witness says: 'For the wages of sin is death,. . .' (Romans 6:23).

*In the Name of Allah, the Compassionate, the Merciful.*

# 5. The Books of God

## WHAT ARE THE MUSLIM SCRIPTURES?

Adam was the first person to receive guidance from God. After he had shown sorrow for his sin (as discussed in the previous chapter), he was forgiven, and at the same time God promised to give Adam guidance. He sent Adam to earth to serve as God's *khalifa*, and appointed Adam as His first messenger to give guidance to his children and the rest of mankind.

No sooner were Adam and his children settled on earth, than Satan started playing his evil tricks again. But whenever chaos, confusion, or evil filled human society, God sent a message for the reform of society. This message was often contained in the Holy Books (Scriptures), which were revealed to His prophets and messengers. However, not all prophets and messengers were given Holy Books. God revealed His Divine Books only to some of these prophets and messengers.

As Muslims it is a central part of our faith to believe in the four Holy Books (Scriptures) of Allah. All these four books are holy and originate from God. They are inscribed on eternal tablets in heaven. Exact copies of these Divine, heavenly Scriptures have been sent down from God (*tanzil*) from time to time. These revealed Scriptures consist of four Books. They have much in common, and all four Books have the same purpose; they are to reform mankind. They confirm one another. Muslims are required to accept and believe in them completely. There is also a fifth Book of God, which as you will note in the following list, is not available, for it has been lost.

*The books are:*

**The Suhuf** (Scrolls) These were ten Holy Scriptures revealed to the Prophet Ibrahim (Abraham) (PBUH), but unfortunately they are now extinct and not traceable in the existing world literature.

**The Taurat** (Torah) This was a Holy Book revealed to the Prophet Musa (Moses) (PBUH).

The Zabur (Psalms) This Holy Book was revealed to the Prophet
                    Daud (David) (PBUH).
The Injil (Gospels) This was a Holy Book revealed to the Prophet
                    Isa (Jesus) (PBUH).
The Qur'an (Koran) This is the Holy Book (final message) to
mankind which was revealed to the Prophet Muhammad (PBUH).

## The Qur'an and previous scripture

As Muslims, our humble submission on the previous Books, which
were revealed before the Qur'an, is a simple one. God would send
a fresh message (revelation) whenever the faith of the people was
in decline. The message would urge people to repent and renew
their covenant (submission) to the will of Allah. We further
acknowledge that God revealed these previous Books to His
prophets for the guidance of mankind. The Qur'an, like other
Divine Books before it, is not a new and strange revelation. Far
from it! The Qur'an is just the final revelation, which confirms
earlier Scriptures, clears up all uncertainties, and perfects the
truth. The Qur'an testifies that there has been earlier revelation
before it. It says:

He hath revealed unto thee (Muhammad) the Scripture with
truth, confirming that which was (revealed) before it, even as
He revealed the Torah and the Gospel aforetime, for a guidance
to mankind (Qur'an 3:3–4a).

The Qur'an really speaks very respectfully of all the prophets
and messengers before Muhammad. Christians and Jews are
referred to as *Ahl al-Kitab*, People of the Book. To these people the
Qur'an admonishes:

Say: O People of the Scripture! Ye have naught (of guidance)
till ye observe the Torah and the Gospel and that which was
revealed unto you from your Lord. . . (Qur'an 5:68).

The Qur'an further encourages Muslims to live amicably with
the People of the Book, and even marry their women. The Holy
Qur'an teaches:

The food of those who have received the Scripture is lawful for
you, and your food is lawful for them. And so are the virtuous
women of the believers and the virtuous women of those who
received the Scripture before you (Qur'an 5:5).

The previous Divine Scriptures (Books) having been revealed by Allah, naturally taught man righteousness, love, and the way of life that is most pleasing to Allah. (However, some of their commands and teachings seem to have been confined to a particular tribe, community, or nation, and to a specific period) *How much more the Quran*

Furthermore, Muslims are aware that human imperfections seem to be included in the Bible. For example, the personalities of the Biblical prophets form part of the content of Biblical Scriptures. Moreover, the Biblical Scriptures include both history and the *Re* Word of God. The Bible seems to be a mixture of history and *History* revelation. Therefore, it is extremely difficult to separate the true revelation in the Bible from the history and the human personality which the Bible also contains/

Therefore, the Qur'an, as the final revelation, is the perfection and culmination of all the truth contained in the earlier Scriptures (revelations). Though sent in Arabic, it is the Book for all times and for all mankind. The purpose of the Qur'an is to guard the previous revelations by restoring the eternal truth of Allah. The Qur'an is the torch-light by which humanity can be rightly guided onto the straight path.

### The nature of the Holy Qur'an

The Qur'an is a unique Book of Divine guidance. The Qur'an is the very Word of Allah. It was revealed to the Prophet Muhammad (PBUH), through the archangel *Jibril* (Gabriel) from an archetype preserved in the seventh heaven. 'Nay, but it is a glorious Qur'an on a guarded tablet' (Qur'an 85:21–22). The Prophet Muhammad (PBUH) was the instrument chosen by Allah for the revelation of His Word. Every letter, word, content form, and meaning of the Qur'an is Divinely revealed. What is especially surprising is that the Qur'an was revealed to Muhammad who was unlettered.

The revelations began in this way. The Prophet Muhammad (PBUH) used to retire to a cave in Mount Hira a few miles outside Mecca (Makkah) for spiritual meditation. One night while at the Mount, he was suddenly awakened by the angel *Jibril*. The angel commanded him to recite (*Iqra*)! The Prophet, who was overtaken by fear, told the angel that he did not know how to read. The angel repeated the command and received a similar answer. Finally the angel pressed the trembling **Muhammad (PBUH)** and taught him to read the following:

Read: In the name of thy Lord who createth,
Createth man from a clot.
Read: And thy Lord is the Most Bounteous,
Who teacheth by the pen,
Teacheth man that which he knew not (Qur'an 96:1–5).

With the above words, the revelation of the Holy Qur'an had
begun. The Divine Messenger from God gave the Prophet the
power to retain and receive Allah's Book. That was about the
year (A.D. 610,) and the Prophet was about forty years old. The
Qur'an was revealed portion by portion for a period of twenty-
three years, which ended shortly before the Prophet's death in,
A.D. 632. The last verse to be sent by Allah said: 'This day have I
perfected your religion for you and completed My favour unto you,
and have chosen for you as religion AL-ISLAM' (Qur'an 5:3).
Between the first and last verses mentioned, the greatest Book in
history was revealed to mankind.

The Qur'an is the most widely read book ever written. Muslims
use it in worship, and it is the textbook from which all Muslims
learn to read Arabic. It is the central reality in Islamic life. The
Qur'an (a name derived from the word 'recite') is different from
any other book. It is divided into 114 chapters (*surahs*), eighty-six
of which were revealed to the Prophet while he was at Makkah,
and twenty-eight at Madinah. The chapters are divided into *ayat*
(verses), all of varying length. The three shortest *surahs* (103, 108,
110) have three verses each, while the longest *surah*, *al-Baqqara*
(2), is divided into 286 verses. Every detail about the Qur'an has
been carefully studied and recorded. For instance, it is known
that the Qur'an contains 6,239 verses, 77,934 words, and 323,621
letters. It has also been recently discovered that the Qur'an is a
mathematical miracle, all of it being based on multiples of the
figure 19* ('. . over it are nineteen' Qur'an 74:30).

A stranger to the Qur'an would be struck by what appears as a
kind of incoherence from the human point of view. Unlike all other
books, the Qur'an does not contain information, ideas, or arguments about specific themes that are arranged in a literary or
serial order. Subjects are not discussed under specific topics. They
are scattered all over the book. Yet to those who first received the
revelation, there was no incoherence, because it was relevant to

---

*Ahmad Deedat *Al-Qur'an: the Ultimate Miracle*, Durban 4001, Islamic Propagation Centre, Madressa Arcade, 1979, pp. 1–75.

their particular situation.

There is no subject which the Qur'an does not discuss. Theology, jurisprudence, science, and history are some of the major subjects the Qur'an deals with. That is why for many centuries, the Qur'an has been the scientific manual and the text book for acquiring liberal education in the Muslim world. Although the Qur'an does not describe all aspects of knowledge in complete detail, it is nevertheless the source and foundation of all true wisdom and knowledge. It is Allah's Word.

Although the Qur'an's is not arranged in a chronological order, the arrangement was determined by Allah's will. This further emphasizes the Qur'an uniqueness. Strangers to the Qur'an would benefit more if they realized that the Qur'an, being a Divine Book, is not to be compared with any form of human writing. It is a unique book whose literary style is quite different from all other known forms of literature. The subject it deals with is man; the central theme is the exposition of reality; the aim of the revelations is to invite man to the straight path of true guidance, which he has lost through time, negligence, and other forms of evil. Anyone who studies the Qur'an, with the above three aspects (subject, central theme, and aim) in mind, discovers that there is no incoherence or any other short-coming in the literary style of these Divine Scriptures.

Furthermore, the Qur'an is the most excellent Arabic poetry and prose ever written or recited. When the unbelievers asked the Prophet Mohammad (PBUH) for proof that the Qur'an is the Word of Allah, he challenged them to produce only one verse or a line of Arabic of equal quality. None could meet his challenge. The Qur'an says:

> And if ye are in doubt concerning that which We reveal unto Our slave (Muhammad), then produce a surah of the like thereof, and call your witnesses beside Allah if ye are truthful (Qur'an 2:23).

The unexcelled excellence of Qur'anic Arabic is one of the proofs of its Divine origin (Qur'an 12:2).

## Compilation of the Qur'an

Whenever the Prophet received a revelation, he memorized it before the angel *Jibril*. After ascertaining its proper recitation, *Jibril* told him in which order to place it. Then the Prophet instructed his scribes (for he did not know how to read or write) to record it under his supervision. Every recording was recited back for his verification. So the Prophet himself directed the proper recording and arrangement of the Qur'an as commanded by Allah. Soon the Qur'an was memorized by the companions of the Prophet for purposes of worship and interest. The Arabs, who had a warm taste for literature, found in the Qur'an a wonderful masterpiece of literature. By the death of the Prophet, the Qur'an had already been preserved in people's memories and on various recording materials such as clay tablets, bones, the bark of trees, pieces of pottery, and stone.

In A.D. 632, after the death of the Prophet Muhammad (PBUH), Abu Bakr became the first Caliph (successor to the Prophet). Umar persuaded Abu Bakr to compile the Qur'an into one volume, because many memorizers of the Qur'an (*Hafiz*) were disappearing from the scene through battles and natural death. Abu Bakr instructed Zaid Ibn Thabit, Muhammad's chief scribe of revelations, to collect and compile the entire Qur'an in the same order as authorized by the Prophet. This he did under close supervision and the help of the companions of the Prophet, who had memorized the entire Qur'an. The final version was checked and approved by all Muslims, who had heard the Qur'an from the Prophet. The Qur'an was still fresh in their memories as it was recorded into book form only two years after the death of the Prophet Muhammad (PBUH).

During the rule of the third Caliph, 'Uthman, it was reported that the Qur'an was being pronounced with different accents, especially by the non-Arab converts to Islam. 'Uthman's action was instantaneous. He recalled all copies of the Qur'an in circulation, and appointed a committee of four former scribes, including Zaid Ibn Thabit, to study the Qur'an further. The committee authorized one standard copy, which followed the dialect of the Quraish, which the Prophet himself had used. The Qur'an used today is the very same one as received by the Prophet, and authorized by Caliph 'Uthman and the companions (*sahaba*) of the Prophet in A.D. 651. No word, order, or punctuation mark has been changed, omitted, or added. Even God testifies to the purity of the Qur'an when He says: Lo! We, even We, reveal the Reminder, and lo! We verily are its Guardian (Qur'an 15:9).

**Hadith**

Islam can be understood through two main sources: (1) The Holy

Qur'an (2) the collections of the recorded words, actions, and sanctions of the Prophet Muhammad (PBUH). These acts (*sunnah*) and sayings (*hadith*) of the Prophet are collectively known as the *Hadith*.

The *sunnah* (acts), and *hadith* (sayings) show the way of life of the Prophet Muhammad (PBUH). '*Sunnah*' means the practices and way of life of the Prophet, and '*hadith*' means the reports of what the Prophet taught or said. The collection of writings known as the *Hadith* include both '*sunnah*' and '*hadith*.' A report or verbal tradition transmitted by word of mouth about what the Prophet said, did, or how he reacted to others (*sunnah* or *hadith*) is called a *hadith* and the written collection are called the *Hadith*. When a companion of the Prophet saw him do something, e.g. praying, he reported it to his friends, who in turn reported it to others, and thus the report continued. Many companions tried to write down *hadith* for their own custody, but they were stopped by the Prophet lest they confuse them with the Qur'an.

Later the science of *hadith* was developed, whereby collections of *hadith* were compiled. In this case each report had to be prefaced by a chain of narrators (*isnad*), who were known to be mature, pious, intelligent, and reliable. The text (*matn*) which the narrators transmitted also had to be intelligible and credible. The process of collecting the *hadith* was practically completed during the second century of the Muslim era. As a result of the exercise, we now have well documented books with all the necessary information about the Prophet Muhammad (PBUH).

The *Hadith* is not a Holy Book (revelation) as the Qur'an and the previous Scriptures. However, to the Muslims the importance of *Hadith* ranks only second to the Holy Qur'an. The *Hadith* is complementary to the Qur'an. It helps to explain and clarify the Holy Qur'an and to present the Qur'an in a more practical form. The Qur'an witnesses thus: 'Whoso obeyeth the messenger obeyeth Allah' (Qur'an 4:80). (Also 33:21, 7:157, 14:44.) As Muslims, our knowledge of Islam would be incomplete and shaky if we did not study and follow the *Hadith*. Similarly an outsider cannot understand Islam if he ignores the *Hadith*.

Muslims believe that God revealed His Word to some of His prophets and messengers for the guidance of mankind. All revelation, which has given guidance to man, needs to be renewed whenever the faith of a people is in decline. These revelations have come to us in the form of Holy Books. All the previous Books revealed by God must be accepted as true. However, the Qur'an is the final revelation, which confirms earlier Scriptures and perfects the truth. The *Hadith*, though not a Holy Scripture, is complementary to the Holy Qur'an.

## A CHRISTIAN RESPONSE

Christians and Muslims are a people of Scripture. Both have an exceedingly high regard for the Word of God. Muslims respect the Bible in its original form with special mention of the *Taurat* (Torah) of the Prophet Moses, the *Zabur* (Psalms) of the Prophet David, and the *Injil* (Gospel) of Jesus the Messiah. All three of these Scriptures are contained in the Bible. The value which Muslims place on these Scriptures is revealed in the Qur'anic warning to Christians and Jews that they should not hide their Scriptures, but rather make their Scriptures available to mankind (Qur'an 3:71). Christians are thankful for the deep Muslim respect for the Bible.

Nevertheless, Muslims and Christians should reflect carefully together on the nature and meaning of revelation. Does not all Divine revelation have an incarnational quality? Is not God's revealed Word to mankind always expressed through human personality, in human language and thought forms? Furthermore, we need to ask ourselves what the criteria are for determining which books are truly the revealed word of God.

Christians believe that the central fact of Divine revelation is God's Self-disclosure. God reveals Himself pre-eminently through His acts in human history. Divine Scriptures are, therefore, a revelation of God's Self-disclosure, and the Divinely inspired record of man's response to God's Self-disclosure. Christians do not perceive of revelation as Divine Books which have been sent down from heaven, but rather as the personal Word of God engaged in lively, active encounter with man. That is the nature of Biblical revelation.

Christians believe that it is exceedingly important to receive and believe the message of the entire Bible. It is necessary to read the entire Bible so that we can receive God's message to mankind. Christians do not believe that some Books are revealed for a particular people for a particular time. Jesus the Messiah used the Holy Writings of many prophets in His preaching, and urged His followers to 'search the Scriptures'. All inspired Scripture belongs together. Each portion of the Bible is needed in order to understand God's full revelation to mankind. Furthermore, no portion of Divine Scripture contains all the truth we need to know.


## A MUSLIM CLARIFICATION

Muslims must and do believe in all the original Books of God which have been revealed to mankind. Muslims also believe that all the universal aspects of previous revelations have been summarized in the Qur'an; in the Qur'an all the universal aspects of Divine guidance have been preserved exactly as revealed to the Prophet Muhammad (PBUH).

*In the Name of Allah, the Compassionate, the Merciful.*

# 6. The Prophets

## THE MUSLIM UNDERSTANDING

Muslims usually make a distinction between a 'Prophet' and a 'messenger' of Allah. The messenger (*rasul*) is sent with Divine Scripture to guide and reform mankind; he is given a Divine Book. The prophet (*al nabbi*) carries information or proclaims Allah's news. The prophets are not given Books like the messengers. Although all messengers are prophets, not all prophets are messengers. Both a messenger and a prophet are people chosen by God to deliver His message, which is given by means of Divine revelation (*Wahy*). This Divine message is for the guidance of a group of people, a nation, or the whole of mankind.

### The nature of Prophets

Allah has bestowed the important office of prophethood on some of His servants according to His wish. They were chosen to guide their communities and mankind onto the straight path of Allah. They all brought essentially the same message—Islam. God gave them greater knowledge about His will, His religion, the human heart, and about good and evil. They guided mankind, taught him to live happily in this world, and to be prepared for life after death.

All Prophets were human beings. They could eat, drink, walk, sleep, speak, breathe, suffer, and face problems like all of us do. They were intelligent, trustworthy, knowledgeable, and most obedient to God. They were the best examples of moral trust, as the Qur'an says: 'It is not for any Prophet to deceive (mankind) ...' (Qur'an 3:161). Allah protected them from serious sins and bad diseases.

It is because the prophets were human that their witness was received with mixed feelings, and even total rejection, amongst their own communities. The Qur'an says: 'And naught prevented mankind from believing when the guidance came unto them save that they said: Hath Allah sent a mortal as (His) messenger' (Qur'an 17:94)?

As Muslims we must not make the mistake of condemning any of Allah's prophets as imposters or uplifting any into a superhuman being. The Prophet Muhammad (PBUH), like other prophets before him, emphasized his human nature. The Qur'an testifies thus: 'Muhammad is but a messenger, messengers (the like of whom) have passed away before him...' (Qur'an 3:144). In another verse Allah says: 'Say: I am only a mortal like you My Lord inspireth in me that your God is only One God...' (Qur'an 18:111). Muslims must have faith in all Allah's prophets. Denying the prophethood of any one of them constitutes disbelief.

As already observed, God sent a large number of prophets at various stages of history for the proper guidance of mankind. These prophets were raised from among almost every people as is witnessed by the Qur'an: 'And verily We have raised in every nation a messenger (proclaiming): Serve Allah and shun false gods...' (Qur'an 16:36). The Qur'an further states:

Say (Muslims): We believe in Allah and that which is revealed unto us and that which was revealed unto Abraham, and Ishmael, and Isaac, and Jacob, and the tribes, and that which Moses and Jesus received, and that which the Prophets received from their Lord. We make no distinction between any of them, and unto Him we have surrendered (Qur'an 2:136).

The exact number of Allah's Prophets is not clear, but Muslim tradition has put it at 124,000. The Qur'an mentions only twenty-five prophets, but Muslims must believe even in those not mentioned. Allah says: 'And messengers We have mentioned unto thee before and messengers We have not mentioned unto thee...' (Qur'an 4:164).

The following are the names of those prophets mentioned in the Holy Qur'an: Adam, Saleh, Lut (Lot), Hud, Y'acub (Jacob) Ibrahim (Abraham), Yunus (Jonah), Musa (Moses), Daud (David), Al-Ya'sa (Elisha), Zakara (Zachariah), Dhul-Kifl (Ezekiel), Isa (Jesus), Nuhu (Noah), Shu'aib, Ismai'il (Ishmael), Yusuf (Joseph), Ishaq (Isaac), Harun (Aaron), Sulaiman (Solomon), Yahya (John the Baptist), Ayyub (Job), Ilyas (Elijah), Idrees, Muhammad (Peace Be Upon All of Them).

Muhammad (PBUH) is the last prophet and messenger of Allah. His mission was for the whole world and for all times.

## The role of Prophets in history

Adam, the first man on earth was also the first prophet of Allah. God revealed the religion of Islam to Adam which is submission to the one true God, the Creator, the Sustainer of the world, the Lord of the universe and the Master of the day of judgement. God made it clear to Adam that man should worship and obey only Allah, the most Exalted. This is the covenant of submission which God gave to Adam: God the Master, and man the servant (*abd*).

Some of Adam's offspring who were righteous followed Allah's teaching, but others drifted into evil activities. They compromised the true guidance by associating Allah with other gods and objects. In order to provide man with firm and constructive guidance, God raised prophets among every people. The fundamental message proclaimed by all prophets was the same. They taught or reminded man of the unity of God, the reward of leading a good, pious, and peaceful life, the day of judgement, and the terrible punishment for unbelievers. All prophets brought this same message (Islam) from Allah. They set very good examples with their own lives. They had to demonstrate by practice the faith which they followed.

The prophets tried to establish a divinely sanctioned moral code, social justice, and co-operation among their fellow men, i.e. a complete way of life. In the process of establishing God's command on earth, some prophets were successful and others were not. Many people were intolerant of God's prophets. They mistreated the prophets by punishing them, torturing them, and refusing to listen to or accept their teachings. Despite opposition, the prophets never gave up or compromised Allah's truth, and their mission was not a complete failure.

Some of the prophets are especially noteworthy. For instance, the Prophet Ibrahim's (Abraham) major achievement was the proclamation of the oneness of Allah. This is a belief man has maintained for several thousand years. Islam acknowledges the Prophet Musa (Moses) as the one to whom Allah spoke: 'And Allah spake directly unto Moses' (Qur'an 4:164); Moses is given the title '*Kalim-ullah*', which means the one to whom God spoke. Nevertheless, important as Moses' message was, his people believed the guidance was intended only for them. They have also added too many ritualistic details to the original law of Moses. Like all prophets before him, Isa (Jesus) son of Mary preached the oneness of Allah. The Christians received the universal message of God, but have compromised it by stressing the 'trinity' instead of the 'unity' of Allah.

At last God has sent His final guidance to all mankind through the Prophet Muhammad (PBUH). The truth that all the previous prophets had proclaimed to humanity was perfected by the Prophet Muhammad (PBUH). The Qur'an, which is Allah's final guidance to mankind, was revealed to the Prophet Muhammad (PBUH), the seal of all prophets, six hundred years after the Prophet Isa (Jesus) (PBUH). Muhammad (PBUH) is the one prophet who fulfilled Allah's mission during his life time. The last message from Allah to Muhammad said: '. . . This day have I perfected your religion for you and completed My favour unto you, and have chosen for you as religion AL-ISLAM. . .' (Qur'an 5:3). So, Muhammad (PBUH) was Allah's last messenger through whom the original religion of man—Islam—was completed and perfected, and a community of Muslims established.

Muslims believe in and respect all the prophets of God who preceeded Muhammad (PBUH). They all brought a uniform message—Islam—from Allah. Muhammad is the last and the seal of prophethood. Through him, Islam was completed and perfected. As he brought the last and latest guidance for all mankind, it is he alone to whom Muslims turn for guidance.

## A CHRISTIAN RESPONSE

Both Muslims and Christians believe in prophets. The writings and teachings of at least thirty prophets and apostles are included in the Bible. The names of many of the Biblical prophets are mentioned in the Qur'an. Moses is one of the greatest prophets of the Bible.

It would be good for Christians and Muslims to reflect together on the meanings of God's encounter with Moses at the burning bush, an event which both the Bible and the Qur'an describe. In this event we recognize that God talked with Moses. It is out of this encounter that the Biblical record reveals a new name for God: I AM, which is *Yahweh* in the Hebrew language. Beginning with the Prophet Moses, God progressively revealed Himself as *Yahweh*—the God of covenant fellowship, the One Who encounters man personally. In order to get the full picture of God's self revelation as *Yahweh* within the Biblical prophetic witness, it is necessary to open our lives to the total prophetic witness.

The message of the prophets is like a great and beautiful building. The early prophets such as Abraham and Moses laid a foundation for the building. Later prophets such as David and Isaiah formed the walls of the building. The Prophet Jesus, the Messiah, is like the roof on the building. All the Biblical prophets taken together form a beautiful building. Christians earnestly and humbly give witness that all people should read and accept the message of all the true prophets of God. Every part of the building is important. All are needed in order to understand God's full revelation to mankind.

## A  MUSLIM  CLARIFICATION

From a Muslim perspective, it is advisable not to carry the event of the Prophet Moses (PBUH) and the burning bush too far. Although God spoke to the Prophet Moses (PBUH) from the burning bush, some Muslim scholars believe that it was the Angel *Jibril* who was present in the bush. At the same time Muslims would affirm that the name 'Allah' is the most profound revealed name for the Almighty. Muslims would witness that we cannot do better than to refer to God by that name of surpassing beauty which He Himself has revealed to the last Prophet, Muhammad (PBUH).

*In the Name of Allah, the Compassionate, the Merciful.*


# 7. The Seal of Prophets

## THE MUSLIM WITNESS CONCERNING THE PROPHET MUHAMMAD (PBUH)

Muhammad* was born in the commercial city of Makkah (Mecca), Arabia, on 12 Rabi Awwal (or Monday 20 August) A.D. 570. His mother was Amina bint Wahab who hailed from Madinah (Medina). His father, Abdallah, was one of the many sons of Abdul-Muttalib, who was the head of the noble family of Banu Hashim, a branch of the Quraish tribe. Abdul-Muttalib was also the chief guardian of the sanctuary of the *Ka'bah*, which is the House of God in Makkah, wherein the sacred black stone is located.

As a child, Muhammad (PBUH) was unfortunate. His father had died a few months before his birth. At the age of six he lost his mother. Then his grandfather, Abdul-Muttalib, took care of him, but he too died only two years later. So, at the age of eight, Muhammad (PBUH) was a complete orphan. However, relatives interested in Muhammad (PBUH) were not lacking. He was soon taken over by his uncle, Abu Talib, son of Abdul-Muttalib. The uncle loved his nephew very much. He gave him good care and protection.

Muhammad (PBUH) spent the early years of his youth with his uncle. He helped him with his work enthusiastically. Muhammad (PBUH) loved and appreciated work; He could do work of any kind without any ill feelings. He mended his clothes and shoes. He tended sheep, goats, and camels, and accompanied his uncle on caravans. He travelled to Syria twice, the first trip being made when he was only twelve. Muhammad (PBUH) had no formal schooling. He did not know how to read and write. Nevertheless, as a youth he was respected and admired by the natives of Makkah for his uprightness, honesty, and good behaviour. Hence, he was given the title, al-Amin (the trustworthy).

---

*The word 'Muhammad' when translated into English means 'the Praised One'.

## The society Muhammad (PBUH) was born into

The society in which Muhammad (PBUH) lived before his mission is called *jahiliyya*, i.e. the period of ignorance and darkness. The Arabs were polytheists with a poor notion of a high god—Allah. They worshipped a pantheon of gods, but the most important ones acknowledged by the Makkahn Quraish were al-Uzza, al-Manat, and al-Lat, who were referred to as daughters of Allah. The *Ka'bah* (the House of Allah in Makkah) had been polluted with all sorts of evil. It was now the home of 360 idol gods symbolizing all the Arab gods, and one was to be worshipped for each day of the year.

Wine drinking, gambling, raiding, and blood feuds were the order of the day. The women performed naked dances and composed poems describing every member of the body. There was no respect for women. Baby daughters were suspected of bringing bad luck and some fathers buried them alive immediately after birth. Property was what mattered, for one's worth was measured by how much one had. This was the society Muhammad (PBUH) grew up in.

Muhammad (PBUH) hated this corrupt society, even as a child. As a man of high moral and spiritual calibre, Muhammad (PBUH) was perturbed by the evil ways and misery of his people. He started frequenting a cave in Mount Hira a few miles outside Makkah for meditation. All the same he continued in employment in order to earn a living.

## Muhammad's (PBUH) marriage

As Abu Talib was a man of scanty means, he looked for a job for his nephew, Muhammad (PBUH). The wealthy merchant contacted was Lady Khadija bint Khuwaylid. She readily accepted to take on the trustworthy Muhammad (PBUH) as leader of her caravans. Khadija was twice widowed with two sons and a daughter. She was extremely wealthy. She found in her new employee an honest, kind, responsible, upright and virtuous man. Muhammad (PBUH) had all the best qualities one could look for.

Attracted by Muhammad's (PBUH) rare qualities, Khadija offered to marry him. He agreed, and a wedding took place. He was twenty-five years old, and Khadija was forty. The couple enjoyed twenty-five years of happy marriage until Khadija's death. Allah gave them seven children, but the three sons died in infancy, and only the four daughters survived. In the end Muhammad

(PBUH) was survived by only one daughter, Fatima, and she lived only six months longer than the Prophet.

After Muhammad's (PBUH) marriage to Khadija, he had more leisure which enabled him to to devote time to his spiritual quest. The Qur'an testifies: 'Did He not find thee an orphan and protect (thee)? Did He not find thee wandering and direct (thee)?' Did He not find thee destitute and enrich (thee)? (Qur'an 93:6–8).

## Muhammad's (PBUH) Prophethood (Risalat)

As earlier stated, Muhammad (PBUH) used to visit the cave (*ghar*) of Hira frequently for spiritual meditation. It was during one night in the month of Ramadhan that he heard a mighty voice commanding him to recite in the name of Allah Who creates (Qur'an 96:1-5). This night of revelation is remembered in Muslim history as the 'Night of Power' (*Lailatu-l-Qadr*). This was about the year A.D. 610, and the Prophet Muhammad (PBUH) was forty years old. The first revelation had descended on Muhammad (PBUH) through the angel *Jibril* (Gabriel). In this way Muhammad (PBUH) was appointed by Allah to be His last prophet (Qur'an 33:40).

Muhammad (PBUH), overcome with fear, hurried home and related to his beloved Khadija all that had happened. She comforted him assuring him that what he had received was true revelation from Allah. She was the first person in Makkah to accept Islam.

The first revelation was shortly followed by a second one, which came to Muhammad (PBUH) when he was shivering and had been covered by a mantle at home. The command was: 'O thou enveloped in thy cloak, Arise and warn! Thy Lord magnify . . .' (Qur'an 74:1-3). Muhammad (PBUH), through Allah's Word, had been chosen to spread His message.

Muhammad (PBUH) began his mission quietly. He preached the oneness of God. He stressed that Allah is all-powerful. He is the Creator of the universe, and the Master of the day of judgement. On the day of judgement the faithful and righteous will be rewarded with paradise, while the unbelievers and the idolaters will end up in hell—an abode of great torture and suffering.

In all Muhammad's (PBUH) teaching, he made it very clear that he was not superhuman or an incarnation of God, but only a human being and a messenger of Allah. The Qur'an testifies to Muhammad's (PBUH) human nature. 'Say: For myself I have no power to benefit, nor power to hurt, save that which Allah willeth . . . I am but a warner, and a bearer of good tidings unto folk who believe' (Qur'an 7:188).

In the first three years, Muhammad (PBUH) had only converted a few Makkans. Important names among them were: Khadija, his wife, Ali, his young cousin, Abu Bakr, 'Uthman, and Talha— all his friends. Soon Muhammad (PBUH) was commanded by Allah to preach in public. He consequently went to Mount Safa, which was opposite the *Ka'bah* in Makkah, where he firmly declared the oneness of Allah. He poured scorn on the idols the Makkans worshipped, and subsequently invited them to submit only to the one true God—Allah. He warned all those who would not submit to God's judgement: 'Nay, but they deny (the coming of) the Hour, and for those who deny (the coming of) the Hour We have prepared a flame' (Qur'an 25:11).

## Opposition and persecution

Muhammad's (PBUH) preaching annoyed many citizens of Makkah. They realized that his preaching would curb their power and economic interests as guardians of the *al-Ka'bah*. They threatened him, but he would not waver. They tried to bribe him with wealth, women, and even kingship, to give up his preaching, but they failed miserably to entice him. Open persecution was the last alternative, and they soon resorted to that. Some of the converts to Islam, like Bilal or Khabbab, were scorched on the hot desert sands with heavy burning stones on their chests. Many Muslims were beaten to death. Even the prophet did not escape persecution. Thorns were spread along his path and rubbish thrown over his back. In Taif, a town to the north of Makkah, the Prophet Muhammad (PBUH) was stoned until he bled.

Regardless of persecutions, more people embraced Islam. As a result of the continuing severe persecution, the prophet advised eleven families to migrate to the Christian kingdom of Abyssinia, then under the rule of King Negus. They were well received and protected. The first group of exiles was joined later by eighty-three others, who included 'Uthman bin 'Affan, who later became the third caliph of Islam. Efforts by the Quraish unbelievers of Makkah to have the Muslims repatriated failed completely. King Negus would not hand over, to the pagan Quraish, the Muslims, who believed in one God, and all His prophets, including Jesus.

Despite the loss of his devout followers, Muhammad (PBUH) continued to preach and get converts. Revelation also continued to pour upon him. About this time, two great figures of Islam embraced the faith. They were 'Umar, who later became the second caliph of Islam, and Hamza, the Prophet's uncle. Umar, who was respected and feared by all the Quraish, started conducting his prayers to Allah in the *Ka'bah*. This stunned and vexed the Quraish, who vowed to increase their persecution of Muslims and their leader.

The Quraish demanded that the Banu Hashim (Muhammad's (PBUH) family) hand him over or face the consequences. The Banu Hashim led by Muhammad's (PBUH) uncle, Abu Talib, refused. Consequently they were boycotted at the valley of Shu'ab-Abu Talib for three years. It was shortly after the trying boycott that Abu Talib died. Though Abu Talib never embraced Islam, he stood firm to the very end in defence of his nephew. As if that was not enough of a blow, at about that time the Prophet also lost his beloved wife, Khadija. The Prophet described this experience as the year of 'sorrow'.

## The Prophet and the Mir'aj

About this same time, a number of people from Madinah who had learned about Islam came to the Prophet in Makkah and embraced Islam. They invited him to come and stay with them in Madinah (then called Yathreb) under their oath of protection. The invitation was welcomed, but the Prophet did not accept it immediately.

In the meantime the Holy Prophet was taken on a night journey (*isra*) to heaven. He was transported from Makkah to Jerusalem on an animal called *al-Buraq*, and then ascended (*Mir'aj*) to the seventh heaven*. *Mir'aj* was a physical as well as a spiritual journey. The Prophet, who had been greatly honoured by Allah, was shown all that was in heaven and the universe. He saw the light and glory of God. This was the greatest gift from God to man.

It was during the *Mir'aj* that Allah commanded the five daily prayers and fasting for Muslims. The Prophet was given the honour of meeting all the earlier prophets and leading them in prayer. This experience gave the Prophet much hope and strength in his year of 'sorrow' in Makkah.

---

*Because Jerusalem served as the earthly station on this wonderful journey, it has remained the third holiest city in the Muslim world.

## The Migration of the Prophet Muhammad (PBUH)

Realizing through experience the Divine guidance that the Quraish were determined to exterminate the Muslims, Muhammad (PBUH) allowed two hundred of his followers to take refuge in Yathreb (Madinah), where they had been already invited. He himself followed later, evading the hot pursuit of the Quraish. He was accompanied by his life companion, Abu Bakr. He arrived in Yathreb on 24 September A.D. 622. This migration from Makkah to Yathreb is known as the *Hijrah*.

The arrival of the Prophet in Yathreb brought great jubilation to the townsmen. In fact, the name of the city was changed from Yathreb to Madinatu 'n-nabi, i.e. the City of the Prophet. The short form is Madinah. Sixteen years later, Caliph Umar designated the year of *Hijrah* as the official starting point of the Muslim era.

The *Hijrah* is a very significant event. The Qur'an teaches:

And when those who disbelieve plot against thee (O Muhammad) to wound thee fatally, or to kill thee or to drive thee forth; they plot, but Allah (also) plotteth; and Allah is the best of plotters (Qur'an 8:30).

Thus the *Hijrah* saw the beginning of a new era.

The Muslims who migrated from Makkah were called the *Muhajirun* (emigrants or followers), and those who welcomed them in Madinah were called the *Ansar* (helpers). The *Muhajirun* and the *Ansar* were now united under the faith of Islam and the leadership of the Prophet. This was how the first Muslim community (*Umma*) was formed. (This will be discussed in another chapter.) In Madinah the Prophet was not only the leader of the Muslim community, but also of non-Muslims. He was now a prophet and statesman, and he continued to receive more revelations, which dealt especially with legislative and administrative matters. For instance, Ramadhan was prescribed as the month of fasting and the *Qibla* (direction of prayer) was changed from Jerusalem to Makkah.

The new community faced many problems, caused by the enemies of Islam. There were enemies who lived among the Muslims and even outside Madinah. Many people treacherously colluded with the Quraish to destroy the Muslims. Given the precarious situation, the Muslim community stood on guard and took strong measures to deal with their enemies.

The Quraish of Makkah, still burning with the desire to exterminate the Muslims, sent their army of 1000 men to meet the Muslims. This was in A.D. 624 (2 A.H.). The Muslims could only field 300 soldiers. The two armies met at Badr, and by Allah's will the Muslims, who were under the inspiring leadership of the Prophet, quickly routed the Makkans. This was a moral and spritual victory for the Muslims.

A year later, the Quraish again attacked the Muslims in the famous battle of Uhud. This time the unbelievers were victorious in battle, but they suffered so many casualties that they could not follow up their victory. In the end the Muslims turned them back. Yet again in A.D. 627, the Quraish attacked Madinah and besieged it. Allah was with the Muslims, for later the Quraish withdrew.

In A.D. 628 the Prophet led 1400 Muslims to his mother city (Makkah) for worship. He made a treaty of Hudaibiyya with the Makkan Quraish. By this treaty, Makkans and Muslims were to be treated on equal terms. Furthermore, the Makkans agreed to vacate the city of Makkah for three days while the Muslims entered for worship. There were many other intricate articles of the treaty. The treaty was very lenient to the Quraish unbelievers.

However, the Quraish broke their part of the treaty, and the Prophet moved on to Makkah with the Muslim forces. He quickly took over without resistence in January A.D. 630 (8 A.H.). On entering the city, he uttered this Qur'anic verse: 'Truth hath come and falsehood hath vanished away' (Qur'an 17:81). He then smashed all the 360 idols that had surrounded the Ka'bah. To his enemies, who were so worried about their fate, he said, 'No blame is on you this day. Go to your homes, for you are all free.* This was a very good lesson for Muslims on how to treat their defeated enemies.

On 23, February A.D. 632 (10 A.H.) the Prophet, accompanied by 14,000 Muslims made his farewell pilgrimage to Makkah. In his last sermon at Arafat, he spoke concerning fifteen social aspects which affect everyone's human relationships. He emphasized the oneness and unity of God, the importance of Allah's message, the day of judgement, the sanctity of life, respect for prophets, respect for women, respect for slaves, and the importance of the Muslim brotherhood. He told the *Umma* that he had bequeathed to them two things: the Book of God and the *Sunnah* (practice) of His

---

*Ibn Sa'd, *Kitab al-Tabaqat*, Leiden, 1330 A.H., Series II, Vol. 2, pp.54–55.

messenger. It was about this time when he received the last
revelation, which we have already mentioned (Qur'an 5:3).

It was exactly three months after the farewell pilgrimage that
the Prophet was taken ill. At exactly noon, on Monday, 8 June,
A.D. 632 (12th Rabil Awwal 11 A.H.), while in prayer, the last
prophet and messenger of Allah died. His death was a trying
moment for all Muslims.

Abu Bakr's comment on the death of the Prophet was well
presented and most effective. To the grief stricken Muslim community, he said: 'If you worshipped Muhammad, he is indeed
dead; but if you worship God, He is alive and can never die.*

## Muhammad (PBUH)—the Seal of Prophets

As already mentioned, the Qur'an and Muhammad (PBUH)
himself made it very clear that he, Muhammad (PBUH), is a
human being. He is neither God nor His son, but just the last
prophet of God who has been sent to show guidance to all mankind.
The Qur'an says:

> Say (O Muhammad): O mankind! I am the messenger of
> Allah to you all—(the messenger of) Him unto whom
> belongeth the Sovereignty of the heavens and the earth.
> ... So believe in Allah and His messenger, the Prophet who
> can neither read nor write, ... and follow him that haply
> ye may be led aright (Qur'an 7:158).

We also learn from the Qur'an that the Prophet Muhammad
(PBUH) has been sent as a mercy to all God's creatures, human
and non-human: 'We sent thee not save as a mercy for the peoples'
(Qur'an 21:107).

Muhammad's (PBUH) message was a logical completion and
perfection of all the previous revelations. God, through the Qur'an
and the Prophet, has emphasized the finality of Muhammad's
(PBUH) prophethood. The Qur'an says: 'Muhammad is not the
father of any man among you, but he is the messenger of Allah
and the Seal of the Prophets; and Allah is Aware of all things'
(Qur'an 33:40). Allah has taught us that Muhammad (PBUH)
has closed (sealed) the long line of His apostles.

Who is able to oppose the Qur'anic teaching? As Muslims we
believe in the Qur'an and whatever it says as the absolute truth.

---

*Hadith recorded by Ibn Ishaq-Ibn Hisham, Serat Rasul Allah, (A Guillau-
me's' translation page 683).

Now that prophethood has come to a complete end, the later ages will need no prophets, but pious men, revivers, reformers, and thinkers.

## A CHRISTIAN RESPONSE

The Christian interpretation of the Prophet Muhammad should be determined by the whole Biblical witness concerning Jesus the Messiah. Christians and Muslims both agree that Jesus is the Messiah. What does it mean for Jesus to be the Messiah? The Biblical witness is that the Messiah is the fulfilment of all the Scriptures and the prophets. Christians believe that He is the Saviour of mankind. The Messiah Himself said, 'I am the Way, the Truth, and the Life' (John 14:6). Therefore, Christians believe that the touchstone of all truth is Jesus the Messiah. That is the Biblical witness.

Therefore, when a Christian looks at the Prophet Muhammad, he needs to evaluate Muhammad in the light of the total Biblical witness culminating in Jesus the Messiah. To the extent that the Prophet Muhammad accepts the total Biblical witness and the central significance of Jesus the Messiah, and to the extent that, the life and teachings of Muhammad give witness to the revelation of suffering redemptive love which we perceive in Jesus the Messiah, Christians should appreciate and affirm the Prophet Muhammad.

## A MUSLIM CLARIFICATION

Muslims do respect the Messiah, Jesus, profoundly, but they do not believe that he is, therefore, superior to all other prophets. In fact, the Qur'an affirms that Jesus foretold the coming of the Seal of the Prophets. The Qur'an says that Jesus came, '. . . bringing good tidings of a messenger who cometh after me, whose name is the Praised One' (i.e. either Ahmad or Muhammad) (Qur'an 61:6).

*In the Name of Allah, the Compassionate, the Merciful.*

# 8. The Umma

## THE MUSLIM COMMUNITY

The Muslim community is called the *Umma*. The *Umma* is different
from any other community. It is not centred on tribe, nationality,
race, or linguistic grouping. The *Umma* does not take its name from
the founder or an event. The *Umma* is the community of Allah.
He is the Absolute Truth to which the Muslim community owes
its life and existence. The life and activities of the *Umma* are all
under His legislative direction. Equally, the life of the individual
member of the *Umma*, both private and public, is under God's
legal command. It is Allah's Law which must be supreme within
the *Umma*. What God has recommended as good for the community, shall always remain good, and what He has forbidden
shall always be denied. The *Umma* cannot authorize negation,
deletion, or abrogation of Allah's supreme Law and scheme of
values.

The *Umma* is divinely established by God, as the Qur'an
witnesses: 'And there may spring from you a nation who invite to
goodness, and enjoin right conduct and forbid indecency. Such
are they who are successful' (Qur'an 3:104). In another Qur'anic
verse Allah praises the *Umma* in the following words: 'Ye are the
best community that hath been raised up for mankind. Ye enjoin
right conduct and forbid indecency; and ye believe in Allah'
(Qur'an 3:110).

This means that the Muslim community promotes virtue and
abhors vice. The community stands for justice and righteousness.
The Qu'ran teaches:

> O ye who believe! Be ye staunch in justice, witnesses for Allah,
> even though it be against yourselves or (your) parents or (your)
> kindred, whether (the case be of) a rich man or a poor man, for
> Allah is nearer unto both (than ye are) (Qur'an 4:135).

Justice is a cherished virtue of the *Umma*. We further learn from
the *Hadith* that one of the greatest *jihads* (striving in the path of
Allah) is the word of justice said to an unjust leader. The *Umma*

is also held together through the principle of unity and equality. The enforcement of the Muslim brotherhood is the greatest social ideal of Islam. The Qur'an states: 'The believers are naught else than brothers' (Qur'an 49:10).

## Muhammad (PBUH) and the Umma

In the seventh capters, we saw how Muhammad (PBUH) migrated from Makkah in A.D. 622, and went to settle in Madinah. Here he was enthusiastically welcomed by the Madinah Muslims, and the many exiles whom he had earlier sent from Makkah. The People of Madinah (especially the Aws and Khazraj who had earlier invited him) were happy that the Prophet had at last come to live with them. The emigrants from Makkah were given the title *Muhujirun* (exiles), while their hosts in Madinah were referred to as the *Ansar* (helpers). The *Ansar* and *Muhajirun* readily accepted the Prophet Muhammad (PBUH) as their head.

The first task, which the Prophet undertook in his new home, was to build a mosque at Quba for the worship of Allah, according to the Islamic principles. This was the first mosque to be built for the *Umma*. It was also the first mosque in history. This marked a turning point in the history of his mission and the *Umma*.

His second task in Madinah was to provide for the *Muhajirun* from Makkah, who had come with scanty possessions. The Ansar shared everything in their possession with the *Muhajirun*. Through this beautiful expression of brotherhood, the lives of the two parties were cohesively welded into one community.

Now that the Muslims were not in immediate danger from the Quraish of Makkah, the Prophet had ample time to organize his new community according to the Divine Law. He created a strong *Umma* in Madinah by Allah's will. During the first phase of the formative period of the *Umma*, the Prophet extended the authority of the *Umma* beyond the circles of the Muslim believers. This was logical because there were a number of people in Madinah under the Prophet who had not yet accepted Islam. The Exiles, the Helpers, and the Jews were the most important groups. To all these three groups, the Prophet granted their status, rights, and obligations.

The Prophet wrote a charter which regulated relationships among the different groups in Madinah. The Prophet's charter is one of the first written constitutions in the world. A thorough understanding of this charter might help one to appreciate why

the enemies of the Muslims were effectively resisted by the *Umma*.
The charter stated:

> 'In the name of Allah Most Merciful, Most Compassionate, this
> charter is given by Muhammad the Apostle of Allah, to all
> believers, whether Quraish or Madinan, and all individuals of
> whatever origin who have made common cause with them,
> who shall all constitute one nation (*Umma*)'.*

The conduct of individuals and the various groups in Madinah
had to be based on this new charter, and the subsequent relevant
revelations. The charter stated that the Jews, who were part of the
Islamic nation, would be protected from all insults and vexations.
They would have equal rights, with the Muslims, and were free
to practise their religion like the Muslims. Even the allies of the
Jews would be given similar rights. The interior of Madinah was
made sacred for all signatories to the charter. But the Jews and
their allies had a duty, like Muslims, to defend the mother city,
Madinah, against all enemies. Any who betrayed the *Umma* in any
way had to be punished. All Muslims were to abhor every man
found guilty of crime, injustice, disorder, or betrayal. The charter
concluded by stating that all future disputes among the people
of the charter would be referred under God, to the Prophet
Muhammad (PBUH).**

In Madinah the mission of the Prophet was remarkably different
from the Makkah period. Muhammad (PBUH) was no longer the
persecuted Prophet; he was now the head of the *Umma*, He was
the chief mediator and chief judge of the *Umma*. Muhammad
(PBUH) never functioned by the conditional authority granted
the tribe, which was typical of Arabian government in the
*jahiliyya*. He ruled, rather, by absolute religious prerogative. The
source of authority was not public opinion, but Allah, who
bestowed it on His Seal of Prophets. The *Umma* was a religio-
political unit—a theocracy. There was no distinction between
what was purely religious and purely political, and there was no
distinction between private and public conduct. Every institution
of the Muslim society, political or social, had to conform to the
Shari'a—the Law of God. It is for the same reason that the

---

*A.A. Galwash, *The Religion of Islam*, Vol. 1, Cairo, Supreme Council for Islamic
Affairs, 1966, p. 94.

**'Al-Medinah', *Shorter Encyclopaedia of Islam*, London, Luzac & Co., 1965, p.294.

Muslim army in Madinah was the army of Allah, and the Muslim treasury was the treasury of Allah.

While in Madinah, the Prophet, who was also a statesman, continued to receive more revelations. The nature of revelation was rather different from that of Makkah. While the Makkan revelations centred mainly on faith, the revelations he received while in Madinah covered a broader range. They dealt with human conduct: food and drink, marriage and family life, morals and manners, peace and war, trade and commerce, contracts, *jihad* (striving in the way of Allah), crime and punishment. At the same time the Prophet exemplified all that he had preached by personal, practical, outward expression of faith and duty.

In Madinah the Prophet established some important institutions. Prayer (*salat*) was to be performed five times a day, preceeded by *adhan* (call to prayer). *Saum* (fasting) was practised in the sacred month of Ramadhan. Friday was substituted for the Jewish Sabbath. The *al-Ka'bah* in Makkah became the *Qibla* (direction of prayer). These practices gave cohesion to the *Umma*, which has never relied upon an ordained hierarchy of priesthood. In Madinah the Holy Prophet created an *Umma* which transcended all ethnic and parochial loyalties.

## Problems of the early Umma

Although the Muslims had succeeded in establishing a state (*Umma*), there were enemies from within and without. The first group of enemies was that of the 'hypocrite Muslims' (*Munafiqun*). These had somehow entered the fold of Islam, but still retained a concealed belief in idolatry. They were tolerated, but when their leader, Abdallah Ibn Ubay, died, the group disappeared. Secondly, the Jews soon showed that they had accepted Muhammad's (PBUH) protection only from motives of temporary expediency. They wished evil on the Muslims, and through treachery colluded with the Quraish of Makkah, who were determined to destroy the nascent *Umma*. The Muslims, aware of the discontented elements in the Madinah *Umma*, kept a watch on their enemies, and at times they had to take effective measures in dealing with them.

In the second year of the *Hijrah*, the Makkahn Quraish fielded a strong force of 1000 soldiers in order to crush the *Umma* in Madinah. The *Umma*, which had the right to defend itself, hastily marched an ill-equipped force of only 300 believers. The armies met at the Battle of Badr eighty miles from Madinah. In the Battle of

Badr the purified army of Allah soon routed that of the infidels, although the infidel army was more than three times the size of the army of Allah. This amazing victory gave a lot of moral and spiritual support to the *Umma*. Justice, truth, and right had prevailed over evil.

Nevertheless, the humiliated infidels of Makkah were still determined to wipe out the *Umma* from Madinah. Twice, in A.D. 625 and 627, they marched against Madinah, and on both occasions failed to destroy the Muslim community. However, despite all these obstacles, the *Umma* succeeded in taking over the whole of the Arabian Peninsula after only a decade of hard struggle.

## The spread of the Umma

By the time of the death of the Prophet Muhammad (PBUH) in A.D. 632, the *Umma* was well established in Arabia. The Prophet had been aware of the universal nature of his mission. The *Umma* was not to be restricted to the Arabs only. The whole world had to get the message of Islam. He therefore made arrangements to send his Muslim envoys to Syria and Egypt. He invited the leaders and their subjects to embrace Islam. The envoys were received with mixed feelings.

As Islam spread, the *Umma*, which was essentially based on Islamic law, was quickly transformed from an Arab *Umma* into a universal Muslim *Umma*. It is not surprising that the *Umma* extended very quickly, after the Prophet's death, far beyond the confines of the Arabian Peninsula. In the process, it brought together peoples of different cultures, races, and nations to form one great *Umma*. Today the *Umma* is still spreading. The universal message of reform (Islam) is now embraced by hundreds of millions of peoples from countries and cultures around the world.

The *Umma*, which was formed fourteen centuries ago, has experienced only two noteworthy sectarian divisions. These have given rise to the Sunni, who are the majority, and the Shi'a. The schism occurred over the problem of leadership for the *Umma*. The Shi'a Muslims believe that the head (*Imam*) of the *Umma* should be a descendant of the Prophet. They have developed a theology of the infallible *Imam*. On the other hand, for the Sunni Muslims, the authority of the community is based on the *Shari'a* which is derived from the supremacy of the Qur'an (*Sunnah*) and the consensus of the *Umma* in all matters. These two sectarian divisions do not detract from the amazing overall unity of the Muslim *Umma*.

The *Umma* is a community of Muslims who completely submit to the will of Allah and strictly follow the teachings of His Prophet, Muhammad (PBUH). The foundation of the *Umma* was laid by the Prophet Muhammad (PBUH) through Allah's will and mercy. The *Umma* transcends all tribal, national, linguistic, and racial loyalties.

## A CHRISTIAN RESPONSE

Christians are impressed with the completeness of the Muslim concept of *Umma*, which includes a total programme for social, economic, cultural, political, and religious organizations. All aspects of life are brought under the rule of the *Shari'a* within the *Umma*. This is an impressive achievement.

The Christian Church also calls on peoples to bring all of life under the rule of God, a rule which Jesus the Messiah proclaimed as the Kingdom of God. Nevertheless, Christians do not believe that the mechanisms of political power can establish the Kingdom of God. Jesus the Messiah showed that the Kingdom of God can never be politically maintained or established. When Jesus was urged by His followers to become a political leader, He refused their request. Through the Messiah, God revealed that it is in redemptive suffering love that the Kingdom of God becomes present in human history.

The Kingdom of God grows quietly. It is the extension of God's love and grace into human society. It is like the invisible yeast in bread, like light in darkness, or salt in food. The Kingdom of God influences cultures and society from inside, but God never imposes His will on people. The Kingdom of God is present whenever people open their lives to the saving grace of God.

The Church, in spite of all its imperfections, is called by God to be a sign among the nations of the presence of the Kingdom of God, a Kingdom of righteousness and peace which transcends all national and cultural systems. It cannot be identified with any religious or political system. It has no geographical or cultural orientation. The Kingdom of God is present wherever people live in a right and joyous relationship with God and their fellowmen.

Christians should confess that we have often misunderstood the Kingdom of God. We have been guilty sometimes of trying to force the Kingdom of God into history. Sometimes we have tended to equate the Kingdom of God with a particular national system or a particular religious culture. This we confess to be a tragic perversion of our calling as Christians, and we should repent.

*In the Name of Allah, the Compassionate, the Merciful.*

# 9. Divine Guidance and Peace

## THE MUSLIM EXPERIENCE

The Muslim desire for guidance is summarized in the opening chapter (*al-Fatiha*) of the Qur'an. It reads:

> Praise be to Allah, Lord of the Worlds.
> The Beneficent, the Merciful.
> Owner of the Day of Judgement,
> Thee (alone) we worship; Thee (alone) we ask for help.
> Show us the straight path,
> The path of those whom Thou hast favoured;
> Not (the path) of those who earn Thine anger nor of those who go astray (Qur'an 1:1–7).

A Muslim is the one who submits to the Divine Guidance which has been revealed by God as a mercy to mankind. In submission there is peace.

### Islam is peace

Islam is the way of peace. The Muslim community, the *Umma*, is the community of peace which has surrendered to the will of God. Anyone can experience peace if he has unequivocal faith in the one true God—Allah—and has completely surrendered to Allah's will and commandments. The submission which is peace includes the faith confession, believing in the Books of God, obedience to the Prophet, and submission to the Law of God. We shall briefly discuss each of these aspects of surrender.

### *The Shahada*

The true believer in Islam must take the *Kalimah* or *Shahada* very seriously—'*La ilaha illa 'llah, Muhammadu rasul Allah*'. The *Shahada*, which states that there is no god worthy of worship except Allah, is the covenant of submission which God has given to mankind. It is the same covenant of submission which all prophets of Allah, from Adam to Muhammad, came to renew.

Pronouncing the *Shahada* must be a sincere confession of deep understanding and appreciation for the one true God, Who is the Creator, Master, and Ruler of all that is in existence in the universe. Only He is transcendent and possesses all the Divine attributes. He is beyond and above all His creation, and to associate anyone in His worship is a grave sin. The Qur'an witnesses:

Or assign they unto Allah partners who created the like of His creation so that the creation (which they made and His creation) seemed alike to them? Say: Allah is the Creator of all things, and He is the One, the Almighty (Qur'an 13:16).

This one true God is also the all-loving, the all-Generous, the all-Benevolent, the all-Merciful, the Compassionate and the most Forgiving. Peace is at the door of all believers who submit to Allah's will, obey His commands and law, and associate none with Him in their worship.

### The Qur'an

As mentioned previously, God has revealed His commands by sending His Books of Divine guidance through His messengers. The Qur'an, as the last revelation, is the final criterion of truth, and all Muslims must submit to its Divine authority. The Muslim experiences peace in grateful submission to the marvellous will of God as revealed in the Qur'an.

### The Sunnah

It is through the prophets that the oneness of Allah and His Divine Books are revealed. Therefore the true servant of Allah must also believe in all the prophets including the Prophet Muhammad (PBUH), the Seal of all Prophets. No one is considered a believer unless he obeys the Prophet, through whom the Qur'an was revealed. The way of the Prophet (*Sunnah*) is the path of Divine guidance. The Qur'an says:

Those who disbelieve in Allah and His messengers, and seek to make distinction between Allah and His messengers, ...Such are disbelievers in truth; and for disbelievers We prepare a shameful doom. But those who believe in Allah and His messengers and make no distinction between any of them, unto them Allah will give their wages; and Allah was ever Forgiving, Merciful (Qur'an 4:150-152).

Allah demands complete obedience to Muhammad (PBUH)

and all of Allah's apostles. Since prophets come with God's guidance, the believer has no alternative except to obey the instructions of these Divinely guided messengers. As for the Seal of Prophets to whom Muslims turn for instruction, the Qur'an remarks: 'We have not sent thee (O Muhammad) save as a bringer of good tidings and a warner unto all mankind; but most of mankind know not' (Qur'an 34:28).

The Prophet Muhammad (PBUH) told the Muslims that they had to follow his instructions in regard to all that he received as revelation from Allah. Muhammad's (PBUH) life was sanctioned as a model life for all mankind. His explanation of the Qur'an was Divinely sanctioned. Muslims cannot make decisions which run counter to those taken by the Prophet. The religious significance of the Prophet Muhammad (PBUH) is summarized thus: 'Verily in the messenger of Allah ye have a good example for him who looketh unto Allah and the Last Day, and remembereth Allah much' (Qur'an 33:21). Therefore, sincere belief in the Prophet and strict obedience to his teachings and example is the one sure way for a Muslim to achieve peace.

## The Shari'a

The Muslim *Umma*, which is the community of peace, must strictly follow God's guidance. This guidance or law is contained in both the Qur'an and the *Sunnah* (practices) of the Prophet. This code of Allah is also referred to as the S*hari'a*, and literally means 'road' or 'path'. The *Shari'a* is the very road, which if properly followed, leads man to peace. The *Shari'a* combines the guidance contained in both the Qur'an and the *Sunnah*, and its very basis is the *Shahada*.

Shari'a (which will be discussed further in another chapter) is the Muslim sacred law. It is the Divine Law. It is the law by which all Muslims must subordinate all their life affairs, both public and private. Rejection of the *Shari'a* is a rejection of the faith of Islam. The *Shari'a* is the ideal pattern for a Muslim's life, and the law which unites all Muslims into a single *Umma*. Strict observation of the *Shari'a* gives man hope of a happy life in this world and the next one. The *Shari'a* is the course through which God has chosen to guide man. Strict adhesion to Allah's code is the way of experiencing peace (Islam) because the *Shari'a* combines all aspects of Divine guidance.

## Personal Ibadat

The submission which is peace is first and foremost an individual effort. Allah, the all-Merciful, the Benevolent, has given man guidance through His prophets and Scriptures. He has done all this to help man submit to the only true source of guidance—Allah. Every believer must strive for submission which is peace.

Belief alone is not enough. Man must practically perform all the duties required of him by the Islamic faith. He must do the *Ibadat* (devotional worship). *Ibadat* is a wide concept, and we have devoted a later chapter to it. Worship involves performing all the primary duties commanded by God and all other good deeds. *Ibadat* is the total experience of complete and unreserved submission to the will of Allah.

Muslims believe that peace is only achieved through total commitment to Islam. Specifically, we mean that peace is experienced through total commitment to the *Shahada*, belief in the Qur'an and Muhammad (PBUH) the Apostle to God, and total devotional submission to the *Shari'a*.

Those who refuse to surrender to Allah's will, cannot experience peace. In fact they experience hell. Allah has said:

> I smite with My punishment whom I will, and My mercy embraceth all things, therefore I shall ordain it for those who ward off (evil) and pay the poor-due, and those who believe Our revelations (Qur'an 7:156).

Through His mercy and justice, Allah will know whom to save from hell. There is no one to help man, except his own upright faith as ordained by Allah and His mercy. Warning man against sin, Allah proclaims:

> Say: I am (relying) on clear proof from my Lord, while ye deny Him. I have not that for which ye are impatient. The decision is for Allah only. He telleth the truth and He is the Best of Deciders (Qur'an 6:57).

## A CHRISTIAN RESPONSE

The Christian witness, like the Islamic witness, invites people into an experience of God's peace. Christians believe that true peace is the experience of a right and joyous relationship with God. The Bible often speaks of 'peace with God'. Christians believe that the t.    .ce with God is the experience of salvation from sin. We beh  e that because of our sinfulness, it is impossible for us to adequately fulfil all the will and commands of God. We believe that our *ibadat* is imperfect and inadequate. Nevertheless, Christians also believe that through Jesus, the Messiah, God has made it possible for all mankind to receive salvation and peace.

The Bible says, 'For it is by grace you have been saved, through faith—and this not from yourselves, it is the gift of God—not by works so that no one can boast. For we are God's workmanship created in Christ Jesus to do good works, which God prepared in advance for us to do' (Ephesians 2:8, 9, 10). The Christian witness is that we receive peace and salvation by faith in what God has done for us through Jesus, the Messiah.

*In the Name of Allah, the Compassionate, the Merciful.*

# *10.* Worship

## THE MUSLIM PRACTICE

Worship (singular — *Ibadah* or plural — *Ibadat*) is submissive obedience to one's Master, God. It is, therefore, the most profound religious practice. *Ibadah* is the confession that Allah is the Lord and Master, and man is the servant or slave. All that the servant does in obedience to God constitutes *ibadah*.

The Qur'an says:

Lo! As for me, my Lord hath guided me unto a straight path, a right religion, the community of Abraham, the upright, who was no idolater. Say: Lo! my worship and my sacrifice and my living and my dying are for Allah, Lord of the Worlds. He hath no partner. This am I commanded, and I am first of those who surrender (unto Him) (Qur'an 6:162–164).

The concept of *ibadah* in Islam is comprehensive. The central point is to acknowledge wholeheartedly that only Allah, the Creator of all things, is worthy of worship. Allah has ordained some aspects of religion (*al-Din*) which constitute particular expressions of worship.

Three obligatory dimensions of Islamic worship are:
   Submission to Allah (*Islam*)
   Belief or faith (*iman*)
   Righteousness (*ihsan*).

The attitude or spirit of right worship includes: prayer (*du'a*), fear of Allah (*khawf*), hope (*raja*), trust (*tawakkul*), aspiration (*raghbah*), remorse (*inabah*), sacrifice (*dhabh*), vowing (*nadhr*), homage (*khushu*), appeal for refuge (*istiaanah*), appeal for succour (*istighathah*), supplication (*istiqanah*), awe (*rabbah*), apprehension (*khashyah*).

All these forms of worship should be directed to no one other than God; true worship is to ensure that all these practices are directly and exclusively performed for Allah. The Qur'an teaches: 'He who crieth unto any other god along with Allah hath no proof thereof. His reckoning is only with his Lord. Lo! disbelievers

will not be successful' (Qur'an 23:117). A worshipper must confess
that God is the only reality. He is the Lord, the Creator, the most
Gracious.

**The right attitude in Worship** (*Ibadat*)
First, we shall discuss several of the right attitudes of worship.
Then we shall briefly discuss the obligatory rituals, beliefs and
practices.

*Fear* is a cherished attitude in Muslim worship. The Qur'an
states: 'It is only the devil who would make (men) fear his par-
tisans. Fear them not; fear Me, if ye are true believers' (Qur'an
3:175). So if you desire good and not evil, fear God in whatever
you do; then you are performing true *ibadah*.

*Hope* and *trust* in God are also important in true worship. A
person who puts all his hope and trust in God in all that he is
doing is performing true *ibadah*. Such a person is raised to great
spiritual dignity which is a great reward. Allah says: 'Who hath
created seven heavens in harmony. Thou (Muhammad) canst
see no fault in the Beneficent One's creation; then look again:
Canst thou see any rifts' (Qur'an 68:3)?

*Remorse* is another important aspect of worship that must be
taken seriously by Muslims. Allah advises Muslims in the Qur'an
to repent and be righteous, before it is too late and judgement is
established. The Qur'an says: 'Turn unto Him repentant, and
surrender unto Him, before there come unto you the doom,
when ye cannot be helped' (Qur'an 39:54).

*Supplication* is one of the most important aspects of Muslim
worship. In the Qur'an we read: 'Praise be to Allah, Lord of
the Worlds, . . . Thee (alone) we worship; Thee (alone) we ask
for help' (Qur'an 1:1–4). This means that Muslims do not only
worship God and ask for His help, but emphatically worship
Him alone and ask for His aid only, for He is the only One
worthy of devotion and able to help man. The Prophet
Muhammad (PBUH) said, 'If you need aid, offer supplication
to Allah'.*

It is *ibadah* for a Muslim to *faithfully fulfill his vows and oaths of
spiritual service*, including service to humanity. If man fulfills his
vows in his commercial and economic dealings, in his contracts,
and in his dealings with all the people he meets, relatives, friends,

---

*Al Bukhari, *Hadith*.

or strangers, all that constitutes *ibadah*. The Qur'an witnesses: 'They perform the vow and fear a day whereof the evil is wide-spreading' (Qur'an 76:7).

*To seek refuge in God* is yet another important aspect of worship. God is the Creator, the Sustainer, the Ruler, and the Master of the day of judgement. God is, therefore, the only Being entitled to man's worship at any time. It is man's duty to worship God by seeking His protection against evil. God protects those who in worship take refuge in their Lord. To this effect the Qur'an teaches: 'I seek refuge in the Lord of mankind, The King of mankind' (Qur'an 114:1–2).

*Sacrifice* is also a significant expression of worship. As for sacrifice, the Muslim witness is quite clear. Sacrifice is not for appeasing higher powers, for God is one. God is not interested in the flesh and the blood of our sacrifices, but only as a symbol of thanksgiving to Him by sharing the flesh of the sacrificial animal with our fellowmen. It is the devotional state of the mind which is important in sacrifice. The Qur'an tells us: 'Their flesh and their blood reach not Allah, but the devotion from you reacheth Him' (Qur'an 22:37). In another Qur'anic verse we are further informed that:

> Lo! my worship and my sacrifice and my living and my dying are for Allah, Lord of the Worlds. He hath no partner. This am I commanded, and I am first of those who surrender (unto Him) (Qur'an 6:163–164).

We have described only several aspects of the right attitudes and expressions of worship. Now we need to consider some aspects of the obligatory rituals and practices of worship.

## The obligatory rituals, beliefs and practices of Ibadah

We have seen that *ibadah* is a means for purifying man's physical and spiritual life. We have described some required expressions or attitudes of worship. In addition to these worshipful attitudes, Allah has also commanded certain obligatory rituals, beliefs, and practices of *ibadah*. We have already noted that these include: (1) submission (Islam) with its pillars of duty; (2) faith (*iman*) with all its articles of belief; (3) good deeds (*ihsan*).

The obligatory acts or rituals of the *ibadah* of duty which make up submission (*islam*) consist of five pillars: (1) testifying that there is no god but Allah and that Muhammad (PBUH) is His messenger; (2) performing prayers (*salat*); (3) paying obligatory alms (*zakat*); (4) fasting during the month of Ramadhan (*saum*); (5) performing the pilgrimage to the Ka'bah (*haj*).

The obligatory beliefs of *ibadah* which make up *iman* are belief in: (1) One God (Allah), (2) His angels, (3) His books, (4) His messengers, (5) the last day, (6) His power (*Qadar* and *Qatha'*).

Finally, the obligatory practice of *ibadah* which makes up *ihsan* (right doing) is to worship Allah as if you are seeing Him, for though you do not see Him, He is seeing you.

It is not our intention to discuss all the obligatory rituals, beliefs, and practices of *ibadah* as outlined above. We are going to restrict our attention to several aspects of *ihsan* (right doing or righteousness) and *salat* (prayer), which is a very important form of the *ibadah* of submission (Islam), because *salat* is an exceedingly important pillar of duty.

### *Right conduct* (Ihsan)

Right conduct is an obligatory form of worship. The *ibadah* of *ihsan* is absolutely essential, because every good deed performed in submission to the will of Allah is indeed an act of worship. Righteousness covers so many areas of our private and public life that we cannot exhaust it here. If a man helps the poor, gives food to the hungry, helps the sick, or performs other similar acts, not from selfish motives, but only to seek the pleasure of God—that is true worship. About righteousness the Qur'an has the following to say:

> It is not righteousness that ye turn your faces to the East and the West; but righteous is he who believeth in Allah and the Last Day and the angels and the Scripture and the Prophets; and giveth his wealth, for love of Him, to kinsfolk and to orphans and the needy and the wayfarer and to those who ask, and to set slaves free; and observeth proper worship and payeth the poor-due. And those who keep their treaty when they make one, and the patient in tribulation and adversity and time of stress. Such are they who are sincere. Such are the God-fearing (Qur'an 2:177).

### *Prayer* (Salat)

*Salat* is the fundamental and most important obligation of *ibadah*. The Prophet is reported to have said, 'Salat is the pillar of Religion

and whosoever abandons it, demolishes the very pillar of religion'.*
On another occasion the prophet described *salat* as, 'the essence
of worship'. It is through prayer that a Muslim totally and
practically submits to Allah.

Prayer is a religious duty. It is *ibadah*. God says: 'Pray unto me
and I will hear your prayer. Lo! those who scorn My service,
they will enter hell, disgraced' (Qur'an 50:60). *Salat* is a fulfillment
of an obligatory duty, an act of homage towards God, a duty
commanded to all the faithful. He who wilfully avoids *salat*
forsakes Islam.

Prayer is the heart and essence of religion. Prayers will be
accounted for first on the day of judgement, before any other
duties. We learn from a *Hadith* that, 'Should one's prayers be
marked as perfect, all his other deeds will win the satisfaction of
the Merciful Lord.'** Because prayer is very important, it is the
first duty imposed by God upon mankind, after believing in His
oneness.

It is prescribed for a Muslim to pray five times a day: before
sunrise, between midday and afternoon, in the afternoon, immediately after sunset, between the time when twilight is over
and just before dawn. The various poses and postures the worshipper makes in prayer are a true embodiment of the spirit of
total submission to Allah. The various recitals strengthen his
commitment to the Almighty God. The frequency of the prayer
is a good lesson for the worshipper in discipline and will—power.
Prayers strengthen the foundation of one's faith and prepare him
for a life of virtue, submission to Allah, inner peace, and stability.
They help to guide man to the most upright way of life, a life of
sincerity, patience, courage, confidence, and hope.

Before a Muslim presents himself before his Lord to offer
prayers, he must be spotlessly clean and pure. The Qur'an states:
'Truly Allah loves those who turn to Him and those who care for
cleanliness' (Qur'an 2:222). Islam takes interest in the purification of the body from all dirt and impurities, as well as purification of the mind from false, wrong, and corrupt beliefs and
attitudes. This purification of the mind, body, and clothes is
called *taharah* (purification). It is only when a Muslim worshipper

---

*Reported by Umar, *Al-Hadith*, Vol III, Lahore, The Book House, by Fazul
Karim, N.D., p. 169.
** Reported by Abi Hurayirah, *Sahih Tirmidh*, Damascus, L-Iftai by Minhaji
Salihin & Izudin Baliyk, N.D., p. 134.

is in the condition of *taharah*, that he can perform the *salat*. The purification of the body can be made through a partial wash of those parts of the body which are generally exposed to dirt or dust, or through a complete bath. The partial wash is better known as *wudu* (ablution), and the complete bath is called *ghusul*. All this proves the importance of *salat* as a form of worship.

It is recommended that prayer be performed in a mosque, and in a congregation if there is one available. This is more true of the *Juma* (Friday) congregational prayer, which is compulsory to all Muslims. On all other occasions, Muslims will also prefer to pray in a mosque if one is available, but if it is not convenient to go to a mosque, Muslims may pray wherever they happen to be, at home, in the market, in parks, at a railway station, in an embassy yard, or on board ship. It is a very common sight to see a Muslim praying by the roadside.

Muslims can perform *salat* anywhere. The Qur'an says: 'And the places of worship are only for Allah...' (Qur'an 72:18). Nevertheless, the common feature which Muslims all over the world must observe, is standing barefooted, all facing towards Makkah (*Qibla*), and conducting the service in the language of the Qur'an. This universal practice of *salat* among all Muslims around the world distinguishes Muslims from non-Muslims. The unity of the world-wide community of Islam is evidenced in the common ritual of *salat*.

We have discussed *salat* as one aspect of the *ibadah* of submission. We have not discussed the other rituals of duty, nor have we probed any aspects of the *ibadah* of *iman* (belief). We have only briefly discussed the *ibadah* of *ihsan* (right doing). But *salat* is a key dimension of the whole experience of *ibadah*, and as such reveals the inner meaning of worship in Islam. In fact, Islam is *ibadah*.

The essence of Islam is *ibadah*. It is in worship, which is a total way of life, an expression of complete and grateful submission to God, that a Muslim gives witness to the reality of his faith in God. Through *ibadah*, the Muslim expresses the submission and peace which is Islam.

From what we have identified as *ibadah*, we assert confidently that there is no Islam without *ibadah*. It is through *ibadah* that Islam is given meaning. It is *ibadah* that provides the pillars of support for the edifice of Islam.

Abu Huraira reports in a *Hadith*, that an Arab came to the Prophet and said, 'Guide me to a deed by doing which I shall enter paradise.'

The Prophet replied, 'Worship God and do not associate anything with Him, observe the prescribed prayer, pay the obligatory *zakat* (alms), and fast during Ramadhan.'

The Arab responded, 'By Him in whose hand is my soul, I shall not add anything to it nor fall short of it.'

When he had left the Prophet remarked, 'If anyone wishes to look at a man who will be among the people of paradise, let him look at this man.'*

So if anyone performs all his essential obligations (*ibadah*), without leaving out any one of them, his place is in paradise. It is through proper worship that man can hope for paradise.

## A CHRISTIAN RESPONSE

The Muslim witness in worship is profound. Right worship is a prominent Muslim concern, and many Christians who have Muslim friends are impressed by the sincerity and devotion of Muslim worship. The Muslim discipline of prayer, fasting, or almsgiving is impressive. Christians appreciate that the essence of Islamic worship is submission to God. As Christians hear and see the Muslim witness in worship, they are often challenged to also become more disciplined in their own experience of worship.

At the same time the Christian witness invites all true worshippers of God to move beyond the mystery of the forms of worship into an actual encounter with God, a personal fellowship relationship with the One, Whom both Muslims and Christians worship. The forms and practices of our worship are less important than the spirit in which we worship. Jesus the Messiah invites us to worship God as our loving heavenly Father. We are invited to worship our heavenly Father in spirit and in truth. We are invited to joyously participate together in the bounty of His grace and love. It is for this reason that eating and drinking in fellowship together in the presence of God (the communion or eucharist) is the most profound symbol and expression of Christian worship; it is a sign of God our loving heavenly Father being graciously present among His people.

As we worship in the presence of God, both Muslims and Christians are reminded that the true worship acceptable to God is a right attitude.

---

*Al-Bukhari, *Hadith*.

## A MUSLIM CLARIFICATION

The fact that Muslims are very concerned about the right forms for worship should not obscure the other fact that a true Muslim should be equally concerned about having a right attitude of total submission to God in his worship. In Islamic worship, the right ritual and right attitude belong together. The third dimension of Islamic worship, *Ihsan* concentrates on right attitude. The Qur'an says: 'It is not righteousness that ye turn your faces to the East and the West; but righteous is he who believeth in Allah (Qur'an 2:177).

*In the Name of Allah, the Compassionate, the Merciful.*

# *11.* Right Conduct

## THE MUSLIM IDEAL

The Almighty God has revealed to the Prophet Muhammad (PBUH) a Divine Law, and a permanent scheme of values. These two are the ideal on which Muslim conduct must be based. First, we shall discuss the Divine Law (*Shari'a*) as the basis for right conduct. Then we shall briefly describe Islamic values.

### The Shari'a: what is it?

*Shari'a* is etymologically derived from an Arabic root 'the trodden path'. It is the 'path' which leads man into submission. *Shari'a* is the Divine Law revealed by God to the Prophet Muhammad (PBUH) for the guidance of the Muslim community. It is the detailed code of conduct for Muslims to follow, both in their private and public lives. It is a well organized system of universal law for right conduct. It is this Divine Law which binds all Muslims into a single *Umma*, even those living beyond the borders of the Muslim nation. This is the *Shari'a*. It is mainly through this universal law that Islam has been able to evolve a civilization, a complete culture, and a comprehensive world order.

### What is contained in the Shari'a?

The *Shari'a* contains every aspect of human action, secular or spiritual. Political, economic, and social affairs are all regulated by the *Shari'a*. The ways and modes of worship, standards of morals and life are contained in the *Shari'a*. Through the *Shari'a*, man receives guidance on how to regulate his life in the best interests of God and himself.

He is given every detail on how to conduct his life, for example, how to deal with his neighbour, his parents, and those under him. While he is commanded to practise mercy, the *Shari'a* also instructs him on how to be merciful in particular instances. The *Shari'a* instructs man on how he should eat, receive visitors, buy and sell, slaughter animals, clean himself, sleep, go to the toilet, lead a government, practise justice, pray, and perform other acts of *ibadat*.

There is no distinction in Islam between private and public conduct, and the *Shari'a* guides man to conduct his total life in line with the Divine Will. Through the *Shari'a*, man can give religious meaning to his daily life. This Divine Law is the right and complete code of life for humanity.

As a complete code of life, the *Shari'a* has clearly shown: what acts of life are compulsory (*faradh*), e.g. prayer; which are forbidden (*haram*), e.g. wine drinking; which are recommended (*sunnah*), e.g. extra prayers; which are discouraged (*makruh*), e.g. eating too much; which are indifferent (*mubah*), e.g. travelling by foot or by horse.

## Sources of the Shari'a (Qur'an and Hadith)

The most important source of Divine Law is the Qur'an. As already observed, the Qur'an is the final perfect revelation. Every word contained in the Arabic Qur'an is from God. As a final revelation, it contains the final and most perfect solutions for all questions of belief and conduct. The Holy Qur'an contains the principles of all the Law. We should, however, not mistake it to be only a book of laws, for it contains other subjects besides law. It is just a very important source of Divine Law.

Although all the general principles of law are contained in the Qur'an, not all of them are explicitly clear in detail and application. They had to be explained and amplified. The natural interpreter for the Divine Law was the Prophet Muhammad (PBUH), through whom the Qur'an was revealed. The Qur'an says: 'They only are the true believers who believe in Allah and His messenger . . .' (Qur'an 24:62). And in another verse the Qur'an continues: 'We have revealed unto thee the Remembrance that thou mayst explain to mankind that which hath been revealed for them, and that haply they may reflect' (Qur'an 16:44). So the Prophet was endowed with Divine wisdom (*hikma*) and authority to preach and explain the Qur'an, as is remarked: 'The messenger hath no other charge than to convey (the message), plainly' (Qur'an 24:54). The prophet elaborated to his community how to interpret and apply the law as revealed in the Holy Qur'an.

When the prophet died, all his sayings and the instructions he had issued (*hadith*), and all his conduct and practices (*sunnah*) were preserved by those who were in his company. These were later rigorously sifted, combined, and compiled into books, e.g. *Sahih Muslim* and *Sahih Bukhari*. These books are known as the *Hadith*.

They are a commentary and supplement to the Qur'an. The *Hadith* writings, which combine both *sunnah* and *hadith*, constitute the second basic source of law after the Qur'an. The prophetic *Hadith* (*hadith* and *sunnah*), as well as the Qur'an, are the infallible sources of law.

Over the years some Muslim scholars (*'ulama*), and especially the doctors of law (*fuqaha*), developed and systematized the *Shari'a*. They used both the Qur'an and the *Hadith* to write the volumes of law which are included in the *Shari'a* today. Two processes were used to determine the meaning of the Qur'an and the *Hadith* when writing Muslim Law. First, the doctors of law relied on the consensus of the Islamic community (*'ijima*). Secondly, they used analogical reasoning (*qiyas*). Both *'ijima* and *qiyas* were the scholarly tools used to determine the practical application of the Qur'an and the *Hadith*. In this manner the *Shari'a* was formed. Over the years four great systems of law developed: Hanifite, Malakite, Shafiite, Hanbalite. These schools of law had different approaches to *qiyas* and *'ijima*. But the Qur'an and the *Hadith* are the source (*madhab*) of *Shari'a* for all the schools of law.

## Marriage

Marriage regulations are an example of the manner in which the *Shari'a* provides perfect guidance. The *Shari'a* gives careful guidance on every aspect of the marriage relationship. In Islam marriage is a solemn contract. Although monogamy is desirable, the moral code of Islam does permit polygamy or divorce under appropriate circumstances. The *Shari'a* carefully regulates every detail of the marriage contract or divorce proceedings. The rights of wives in a polygamous household are similarly defined by the *Shari'a*.

Polygamy has been practised throughout human history. Islam did not ignore this practice nor leave it unregulated. Polygamy has been conditionally permitted, with a maximum of four wives. This conditional permission is not a pillar of faith nor an act of worship. The Qur'an teaches:

> Marry of the women, who seem good to you, two or three or four; and if ye fear that ye cannot do justice (to so many) then one (only) or (the captives) that your right hands possess. Thus it is more likely that ye will not do injustice (Qur'an 4:3).

The maximum of four has been permitted provided they are

treated with perfect equality in material and immaterial things, as well as in affection. Abdallah Yusuf says: 'As this condition is most difficult to fulfill, I understand the recommendation to be towards monogamy.'*

The regulations governing polygamy were not aimed at encouraging it as a necessity or rule. Abolishing it completely, however, was not practicable, so Islam took the practical step of permitting it, but with limitations.

Apart from the *Shari'a*, the second blueprint of the ideal for Muslim conduct is the scheme of moral teachings. Morality is such an integral part of Islam, that moral values are mentioned in almost all passages of the Qur'an. We cannot discuss all of them in this short chapter. Some of those repeatedly mentioned are: sincerity, honesty, humility, chastity, meekness, charity, politeness, love, forgiveness, goodness, courage, sympathy, justice, straightforwardness, obedience, appreciation, kindness, and steadfastness.

The dimensions of morality cover a number of aspects. These are mainly the relationship between man and God, man and man, man and other creatures, and man and his internal self. The moral values in Islam teach man to desist from inflicting injury upon his fellowmen, and also encourage him to do good to others.

The Muslim understanding of moral values can be partly summarized in the following Quranic verse:

Ascribe no thing as partner unto Him. (Show) kindness unto parents, and unto near kindred, and orphans, and the needy, and unto the neighbour who is of kin (unto you) and the neighbour who is not of kin, and the fellow-traveller and the wayfarer and (the slaves) whom your right hands possess (Qur'an 4:36).

The positive morals, which encourage man to do good, stress that man must obey and love the one true God. He must peacefully surrender to the will of Allah. Submission to Allah's will serves as a source for strengthening man's moral qualities. These qualities include kindness and love to his relatives, parents, neighbours, or strangers. He must respect the legitimate rights of others. He

---

*Abdallah Yusuf Ali, *The Holy Quran*, Beirut, Dar al Arabia, 1968, p.179.

should be honest and must fulfill all his commitments, and repent for his sins. He must work for a living.

Apart from those positive moral teachings, which instruct man to submit to the will of God and to be good to himself and to others, there are other protective or precautionary moral values, which help man to abstain from injuring the life or the property of other human beings. Let us briefly discuss some of these moral teachings.

### Chastity

A Muslim is restricted from casting unrestrained looks upon strangers, and must refrain from listening to stories of lust and romance. All sexual relations out of wedlock are forbidden. The Qur'an says: 'And who guard their modesty—Save from their wives or the (slaves) that their right hands possess, for then they are not blameworthy, . . .' (Qur'an 23:5–6).

The manner of dress in public is also regulated by Islamic moral values. The Qur'an states:

> Tell the believing men to lower their gaze and be modest. That is purer for them. Lo! Allah is Aware of what they do. And tell the believing women to lower their gaze and be modest, and to display of their adornment only that which is apparent, . . . (Qur'an 24:30–31).

This restraint (chastity) helps man to attain the highest form of moral values.

### Honesty

Muslims are commanded to be honest and faithful and to care for that which is entrusted to them. The Qur'an teaches:

> Give unto orphans their wealth. Exchange not the good for the bad (in your management thereof) nor absorb their wealth into your own wealth. Lo! what would be a great sin (Qur'an 4:2).

In another verse God says: 'Give just measure and be not of those who diminish; and weigh things with an exact and right balance' (Qur'an 26:181–182). The various Qur'anic teachings help man to guard against all forms of corruption by remaining honest.

## Peace

Islam means submission and peace. Peacefulness is one of the greatest moral values. Muslims are urged to live peacefully with one another. '. . . Lo! Allah loveth the equitable. The believers are naught else than brothers . . .' (Qur'an 49:9–10). Peacefulness means that no one inflicts injury to another person. This is what Islam strives for.

## Politeness

Muslims have been commanded to be polite in all their conduct. They should avoid suspicion and vain talk. To this effect the Qur'an exhorts: 'O ye who believe! Shun much suspicion; for lo! some suspicion is a crime. And spy not, neither backbite one another' (Qur'an 49:12).

## Health and diet

While these four values, chastity, honesty, peace, and politeness are meant to train man to refrain from causing injury to others, there are other values which prevent man from causing injury to himself. Under these moral values, man is prohibited from touching all sorts of intoxicants (Qur'an 2:219, 5:93–94), eating the meat products of swine, wild animals with claws, all birds of prey, dead meat, reptiles, worms, and that which is not properly slaughtered (Qur'an 2:172–173; 5:4). This scheme of moral values has been ordained by Allah to help man develop his character and personality in accordance to Allah's will. These high moral values are necessary for the guidance of man along the straight path.

There is no Islam without profound moral values. It is God's Divine Law (*Shari'a*), and His permanent scheme of moral values, which constitute the blueprint of the ideal for Muslim conduct. The two complement and supplement each other, and the Muslim ideal of right conduct cannot be fully realized in the absence of either.

## A CHRISTIAN RESPONSE

How do we become righteous?

Islam recognizes that rules and moral teaching are helpful in many ways. But the question remains, are moral and civil regulations sufficient?

The Biblical witness says,

Put off your old nature which belongs to your former manner of life and is corrupt through deceitful lusts, and be renewed in the spirit of your minds, and put on the new nature, created after the likeness of God in true righteousness and holiness (Ephesians 4:22, 23).

For no human being will be justified in His sight by works of the law, since through the law comes knowledge of sin. But now the righteousness of God has been manifested apart from law, although the law and the prophets bear witness to it, the righteousness of God through faith in Jesus Christ for all who believe (Romans 3:20–22).

*In the Name of Allah, the Compassionate, the Merciful.*

# 12. The Mission of the Umma

## THE WORK OF THE UMMA

The first two revelations to Muhammad (PBUH) were commands to proclaim. At Mount Hira, God commanded the Prophet to recite in the name of His Lord Who created. By this very revelation, Muhammad (PBUH) had been called to prophethood. The second Divine command said: 'O thou wrapped up in thy raiment! Keep vigil the night long, . . . and chant the Qur'an in measure' (Qur'an 74:1-4). By this second Divine revelation, the Prophet was ordered to start preaching God's message. He was to proclaim publicly the name of the Lord, Allah. Through this revelation, Muhammad (PBUH) was called to be a Messenger of Allah.

### The mission of the Prophet

By Allah's will and design, Muhammad's (PBUH) mission was made logical and successful. First, he was commanded to warn his near relatives, then his people, then the Arabs who were around them, followed by the whole of Arabia, and lastly, but not least in importance, the whole world. The Prophet's mission was to start from known to unknown. Allah says: 'Lo! We have revealed it, a Lecture in Arabic, that ye may understand' (Qur'an 12:2). And in another verse it is stated thus: 'And We have made (this Scripture) easy in thy language only that they may heed' (Qur'an 44:58).

Muhammad stood in Makkah and proclaimed the message from God. He warned unbelievers of the dreadful punishment after the day of judgement. He called the Makkans to submit to the will of God through preaching. The majority of the Quraish received Muhammad's message with open hostility. Muhammad and his retinue of followers were tortured and persecuted. The Almighty Allah commanded him to restrain himself and to be patient. When the persecution of Muslims became intense, the Prophet was advised to migrate by Allah. The Qur'an says:

And when those who disbelieve plot against thee (O Muhammad) to wound thee fatally, or to kill thee or to drive thee
forth; they plot, but Allah (also) plotteth; and Allah is the
best of plotters (Qur'an 8:30).

In Madinah, the Prophet welded his believers into a single
brotherhood, the *Umma*. The Muslims soon discovered enemies
of the *Umma*, from both within and without. It was at about this
time that the Prophet was commanded to fight those who fought
him, and to restrain himself from those who did not make war
with him. The Qur'an says: 'And if they incline to peace, incline
thou also to it, and trust in Allah. Lo! He is the Hearer, the
Knower' (Qur'an 8:61). The Muslims were commanded, from
the very beginning, not to start aggression or hostilities against
other people. They were, however, to stand firm in resisting
aggression and oppression directed against the *Umma* and
humanity.

In promoting the mission of the *Umma*, Muslims are to follow
the teachings and good examples of the Prophet Muhammad
(PBUH). The Qur'an states: 'They only are the true believers
who believe in Allah and His messenger...' (Qur'an 24:62).
Muslims acknowledge that Muhammad (PBUH), as the last
prophet of Allah, was the only prophet who fulfilled his mission
in his life time. The last revelation he received before he died
said: 'This day have I perfected your religion for you and completed My favour unto you, and have chosen for you as religion
AL-ISLAM' (Qur'an 5:4).

By the time of Muhammad's (PBUH) death, he had established
the *Umma* of believers. He had also developed a complete model
of Islam on this earth for mankind to follow. After the Prophet,
the *Umma* took on the honoured work of proclaiming the perfect
message of Islam throughout the whole world.


## The spread of Islam

The Qur'an and the Prophet Muhammad (PBUH) made it clear
that they had a message for all mankind. In many passages, the
Qur'an calls upon the children of Adam or 'mankind' to accept
Islam. The message of the Qur'an is universal, although the
Arabs, who were near the Prophet, were the first to hear it. It is
addressed to all humanity. The Qur'an enlightens people con-

cerning God and His purposes with man. The Qur'an is the
true guide for man in this world, and it gives him glad tidings of
the next world, if he seeks the righteous way of life.

Allah says: 'This is naught else than a reminder unto creation,
Unto whomsoever of you willeth to walk straight' (Qur'an 81:27–
28).

In another verse Allah has described the Qur'an thus: '(This is)
a Scripture which we have revealed unto thee (Muhammad)
that whereby thou mayst bring forth mankind from darkness
unto light . . .' (Qur'an 14:1).

From the start of his mission to the end, the Prophet never lost
track of the universal nature of his mission, whether he was
preaching to relations, Arabs, or addressing the whole of mankind.
This mission is Islam. Islam is total submission to the one true
God, the Creator, the Sustainer and the supreme Sovereign of
all the worlds. Muslims are therefore charged with the noble
mission of bringing the whole world to its supreme Sovereign,
and of freeing it from servitude to any false god. The propagation
of Islam to all people is a religious duty which must be undertaken
by all true Muslims by following the good example of the Prophet
who was sanctioned as 'Mercy for all mankind'.

## Striving in the cause of God (jihad)

*Jihad* (striving) does *not* refer to war as an instrument to spread
Islam. The allegation by some orientalists that Islam is intolerant,
and was propagated by the sword, shows how little outsiders
understand Islam and its mission. (We will not be able to discuss
the allegations made by non-Muslims about Islam, and the
counter statements by Muslims, reminding Christians of the
massacres by Justinian the Byzantine Emperor (A.D. 527–562),
the fearful wars of the Christian Clovis (A.D. 466–511), and the
savage conduct of the Christian crusaders when they captured
Jerusalem—all done in the name of Christianity.) Islam, which is
a complete way of life, makes no distinction between private and
public conduct, between the secular and the spiritual. It is in this
line, that war has not escaped Muslim legislation.

It is mentioned in several verses of the Qur'an that war is part
of life, as long as there is injustice and oppression in the world.
The Qur'an says: 'And if Allah had not repelled some men by
others the earth would have been corrupted. But Allah is a Lord
of Kindness to (His) creatures' (Qur'an 2:251).

In another verse the Qur'an states:

> For had it not been for Allah's repelling some men by means of others, cloisters and churches and oratories and mosques, wherein the name of Allah is oft mentioned, would assuredly have been pulled down' (Qur'an 22:40; see also Qur'an 2:216).

Islam in its practical teachings, has recognized the inevitability of war, and possesses the necessary legislation to regulate war.

Nevertheless Islam does not condone spreading the *Umma* through war. Unfortunately when non-Muslims try to explain why the Muslim faith was embraced by so many people of the world in a relatively short time, the common reason given is that of the holy war or *jihad*. The term *jihad* has often confused non-Muslims and Muslims alike. What is *jihad?* In the Arabic language, the word *jihad* is not synonymous with war. *Jihad* means the exerting of one's utmost power in repelling an enemy. It is a striving in the cause of God.

The struggle in the cause of God is of three kinds. The first is the struggle against a visible enemy. The second is the struggle against the temptations of the devil. The third is the struggle against one's own passions. While carrying on a *jihad*, Muslims must strive with their time, knowledge, energy, possessions, talents, and all their resources for the cause of God. This is the true meaning of *jihad*, which was commanded by Allah, and expounded by the Holy Prophet, for the faithful to follow. It has a much broader meaning than fighting in battle.

We have already discussed when and why the Prophet was ordered to fight. We repeat that Islam has recognized fighting as lawful for only two purposes: self-defence *and* restoration of justice, freedom, and peace. Muslims are commanded not to start any aggression, and not to submit to any aggression, or oppression from their enemies. The Qur'an teaches:

> Fight in the way of Allah against those who fight against you, . . . And fight them until persecution is no more, and religions is for Allah. But if they desist, then let there be no hostility except against wrongdoers (Qur'an 2:190–193).

This is the condition of war in Islam. War is not the mission of Islam nor the normal course for the *Umma*.

**Islam is peace**

Islam is the religion of peace. Its meaning is peace. It is the

peaceful surrender to the will and commands of God. The **Muslim**
salutation, 'Assalaam Alikum' means, 'May God's peace be upon
you'. Islam strives to bring peace in the world. Islam will never
act with aggression against non-Muslims who make peace with it,
or are even indifferent to it. Islam does not force people to accept
it, because it is a faith that must come from the deep conviction
of an individual. The Qur'an categorically affirms this by saying:
'There is no compulsion in religion. The right direction is hence-
forth distinct from error' (Qur'an 2:256). The gracious mission of
the *Umma* is to proclaim the message of Islam peacefully to all
people of the world, and to invite all mankind into the *Dar al
Islam* (region of peace) which is the *Umma*.

In his life time the Prophet Muhammad (PBUH) sent Muslim
envoys to carry the light of Islam to the rulers of the neighbouring
countries. These were namely, Hercalius the Byzantine Emperor,
Chosres the Persian Emperor, Negus of Abyssinia, and Hamza
of Yemen. The envoys were received with mixed feelings in the
various capitals, the worst reception being given by the Persian
Emperor. It was not long before Roman and Persian military
expeditions violated Muslim territory in cross-border raids.
Orders were even given by the Roman court for the Prophet's
head. So, by the death of the Prophet, the Muslims had been
involuntarily dragged into war by their neighbours, which they
(Muslims) pushed to the logical conclusion a few decades later.
In the process of defeating their enemies, the Muslims did not
persecute or force conversion on the local populace.

It should be noted, however, that not every war which Muslims
have fought was in the cause of God. If the Muslims commit
aggression for personal motives, they should know that they are
acting contrary to the true teachings of Islam, and are inviting
Allah's displeasure.

The Muslims followed Allah's command, and the good example
of the Holy Prophet, by preaching Islam to the outside world.
Teachers, merchants, mystics, scholars, and simple laymen, all
participated in the noble task of proclaiming Islam throughout
the whole world. One hundred years after the death of the Prophet,
the name of Allah the Greatest was being praised as far as China
to the east, Morrocco to the west, and France to the north. By
the same time, Islam had made a meaningful presence in East
Africa and North Africa. Today Islam has spread to all parts of
the world. This shows how the *Umma* has been successful and
active in peacefully preaching the perfect message of Allah.

## Mission through service

Since Islam is a perfect way of life, service is another important aspect of the Islamic mission. The Prophet has said: 'He is not a true believer who eats his fill while his neighbour lies hungry by his side.' We have earlier remarked that if one generously helps the poor, the destitute, feeds the hungry, serves the suffering, he has indeed performed *ibadah* (worship). The third pillar of Islamic duty (obligatory alms) is imposed on Muslims to help the needy. Because service is an important duty of Muslims, two Islamic organizations in Kenya, namely the Islamic Foundation and the Young Muslim Association, have set up free boarding schools and orphan homes in North Eastern Kenya. These two organizations are an example of Islamic service ministries all over the world. Muslims are doing their best to fulfill the mission of the *Umma* through service to humanity.

## The Umma and history

It is the will of God that all men submit to the right guidance revealed in the Qur'an and the *Hadith* as explained in the *Shari'a*. Any people who submit to the *Shari'a* are blessed. Although there is no compulsion in religion, and although God Himself recognizes the diversity of religious practices of peoples, nevertheless, now that the final Book from God has been revealed, it is right that all peoples respond to the Muslim witness and submit to the *Shari'a* of Islam. In so doing people become part of the region of peace, the *Umma*.

Muslim scholars are not certain how extensive the *Umma* will become before the end of history. Some believe that before the final judgment, the *Umma* will spread to all nations and peoples, and others believe that in the latter years there will be an increase in unbelief. Nevertheless, according to the *Hadith*, Muslims do believe that Jesus the Messiah will return at the close of history to establish Islam throughout the earth. Then there will be a resurrection and a final judgement in which God will determine who should go to hell and who should go to heaven. Hell is described as a place of fire and eternal punishment, and heaven is a paradise of joy and plenty. The best security against hell is for a person to submit to the religion of peace, the *Umma*, by obeying the *Shari'a* which has been revealed by God to the Prophet Muhammad (PBUH).

Despite problems that the *Umma* has had to grapple with over the last fourteen centuries, it has been remarkably successful in its work. The mission of proclaiming Allah's perfect message throughout the world has been taken seriously, and many Muslim organizations like Rabita (World Muslim League—Mecca), Islamic Call Society (Libya), or Azhar University Mission (Cairo) continue to send missionaries to preach Islam in all parts of the earth. Islam, which has never known an ordained priesthood with an organized missionary backing, has generally been propagated by poor Muslims who have had to sacrifice every bit of their limited human and material resources to serve humanity. Through sacrificial service and faithful preaching, the *Umma* will always strive to fulfill its mission of establishing God's Rule and Law on earth, after the example of Prophet Muhammad (PBUH).

## A CHRISTIAN RESPONSE

Muslims believe that they have a witness to give to the world. The tremendous growth of the *Umma* is evidence that Muslims have given their witness very effectively.

Christians also believe that they have a witness to proclaim to the world. Both Christians and Muslims in their relationships to each other need to recognize that witness is at the heart of their faith. When Muslims live in lands which are predominantly Christian, the Church needs to encourage freedom for Muslims to witness and for Christians to convert to Islam if they decide to do so. Freedom for witness and conversion is a basic God-given right.

Similarly, whenever Christians are in a minority in a land which is predominantly Muslim, the right of the Christians to witness freely concerning their faith should be assured by the Muslim majority. And Muslims should be free to become Christians if they so choose. A Christian community which cannot give free and open witness to its faith experiences great pain, for at the centre of Christian faith is the compulsion and command of God to be a witness. Because human freedom is a basic God-given right, people should have the right to accept the witness which they hear, whether it be a Muslim witness or a Christian witness, or the witness of any other faith for that matter.

Christians deeply appreciate the Muslim insistence that there is 'no compulsion in religion'. We confess that in our Christian history we have sometimes failed to live according to that ideal.

We have sometimes used force to convert peoples to Christianity We confess this sin and repent of it.

Christians also appreciate that ideally *jihad* in Islam is for self protection, and not for aggression. However, when self protection is applied in such a manner as to prevent the Church from being faithful to its witness in the world, this is exceedingly painful. Authentic self protection should also include the willingness to hear the witness of those whom the Qur'an recognizes as being 'closest in affection' (Qur'an 5:82) to the Muslims.

The Bible also affirms, like the Muslim *Hadith*, that Jesus the Messiah will return at the end of history. The Bible explains in considerable detail the meaning of the second coming of the Messiah. It would be very good for Muslims and Christians to explore together the meaning and significance of the anticipated coming of the Messiah at the end of history.

# PART II   THE CHRISTIAN WITNESS

*'O give thanks to the Lord; for he is good; for His steadfast love endures forever* (1 Chronicles 16:34).

# *13.* The Lord God is One

## THE CHRISTIAN WITNESS

Christians believe in one God. The key verse of the Torah* of the Prophet Moses is: 'The Lord our God is one Lord; and you shall love the Lord your God with all your heart, and with all your soul, and with all your might' (Deuteronomy 6:4). God commanded the believers to teach these words to their children, to talk of God when they are at home and when they are on a journey, in the morning and in the evening, to tie these words on their hands or foreheads, and to write them on the doorposts of their houses (Deuteronomy 6:6–9).

### God is one

God is one and He commands us to love Him totally. It is the will of God that He becomes the focus of our entire life. The oneness of God and the command that we should love God is the central teaching of the Torah.

Jesus Christ (the Messiah),** speaking more than a thousand years after the Prophet Moses, was asked: 'Teacher, which commandment is the first of all?' Jesus answered: 'The Lord our God, the Lord is one; and you shall love the Lord your God with all your heart, and with all your soul and with all your mind, and with all your strength' (Mark 12:28–30).

Both the Torah of the Prophet Moses and the Gospel (*Injil*) of Jesus the Messiah agree that God is one. We are commanded to love that one God. Only He has the right to command our ultimate loyalty.

---

*The Torah is the first five books of the Bible: Genesis, Exodus, Leviticus, Numbers, Deuteronomy. The Arabic name for Torah is *Taurat*.

**Messiah is the Semitic term for the Greek term Kristos or Christ. Messiah or Christ means 'The Anointed One'. Because Arabic is a Semitic language, most Muslims are more familiar with the term Messiah than Christ. For this reason we shall generally refer to Christ with His Semitic title: Messiah.

## What God is not

Why does God have the right to command our ultimate loyalty and love? God has this right because of Who He is. But who is God? In order to understand God as revealed in the Bible, it is helpful to look at some negatives first. What is not true about God?

First, God is not the invention of the human mind. He is not the creation of mankind. He is not, as some psychologists suggest, a psycho-projection of the mind. According to the Bible all the gods which man invents are totally false. The Bible calls all man-made gods, false gods or images (Hosea 13:2,3). The one true God cannot be created by man, because only He is the Creator.

Second, God is not in any way a part of nature. God created the world. No aspect of the universe is God; He is other than the creation. This is one reason why the Bible strongly condemns the worship of any graven images. No aspect of creation is worthy of worship. Only God the Creator deserves our loyalty and our worship (Exodus 20:4-6).

Third, God is not a philosophical principle. Philosophers often concern themselves with questions such as the proofs that God exists. Much of western and eastern philosophy concerns itself with questions concerning the unifying principle behind the universe. These are speculative ideas in which the mind of man attempts to decide whether there is a God or not. The Bible has none of this. God, as revealed in the Bible, is the One Who encounters us. He is known, not through human philosophy, but rather by what He does. It is God Who takes the initiative to reveal Himself to mankind. That is Biblical theology.

## God is active

If God is known by what He does, the question then arises, what has He done? We shall look at this in greater depth in later chapters, but let us briefly note three important spheres of God-action:

First, God has acted as Creator. God is the origin of everything. Before creation was, God already existed. He is the originator of all that is visible and invisible. One way in which the Bible refers to God the Creator of mankind is 'Father'. God as Father cares for His creation, and especially for mankind. He has not abandoned the universe. He is always present to preserve and keep what He has created. God creates *and* preserves the universe.

Second, God has acted by revealing Himself from time to time to some of the prophets. God guided the prophets or their disciples to write the revelations which the prophets received from God. It is in this way that the Holy Scriptures have been formed. The Bible often refers to God Who reveals Himself through the words of the prophets as Spirit. The prophets sometimes gave witness that 'The Spirit' came upon them, and then they prophesied (Ezekiel 2:2, Numbers 11:26–30, Zechariah 7:12). God, as the One Who reveals His Word through the mouths of prophets, is frequently called Spirit.

Third, God has also acted in history. His acts in history were especially evident to the people of faith who participated in the Biblical Covenant Community. (Psalm 78:1–72). The Christian witness is that the most dramatic and definitive act of God in human history is the coming of the Messiah, Jesus Christ. Through the Messiah God has revealed Himself in a special way as Saviour (Matthew 1:21).

## God is love

In later chapters, we shall discuss the Christian witness concerning Jesus the Messiah in greater depth. For the present we will only note that the breakthrough into history of the Messiah Event is crucial to the Christian understanding of God as the One Who loves mankind so deeply that He actually suffers when we do wrong. It is through God's action in Jesus the Messiah that the Christian Church recognizes in a special and marvellous way the astonishing affirmation that God loves people. That affirmation is the centre of all that Christians believe and witness concerning God.

Christians believe that through God's revelation in Jesus the Messiah, all the dimensions of God's revelation through nature, prophets, or history are fulfilled and enlightened. Through Jesus we recognize in a most specific and special way that God's revelation to mankind is a drama of self-giving love. That is the key to understanding God as the Father Who is the Creator, God as the Spirit Who reveals Himself through the words of prophets, God as the Saviour Who acts in history (Luke 5:32). The Apostle John, who was one of the closest disciples of Jesus the Messiah, says it simply and profoundly: 'God is love' (1 John 4:16).

The love of God is the fountain of life and truth out of which the Christian witness concerning God proceeds. Christians try to express in word and deed the love which they have experienced. Nevertheless, they know that what they say and do are not an adequate witness. How can a Christian witness truly convey the marvel, mystery, and unity of God as Creator, Spirit, and Saviour? How does one express the awareness that God loves totally, that the very essence of God is love, that even within God Himself there is an ongoing, eternal fellowship of self-giving love, that the very unity of God is bound up in His eternal self-giving love? The Christian witness is that God is one because He is love. The one true God Who reveals Himself as Creator, Spirit, Saviour is a perfect unity of self-giving love (John 17:22).

Although the Bible does not use the term, later in the history of the Church Christians began to use the word Trinity to try to express in human language the mystery of God's perfect unity and perfect love. Tertullian, in early third century North Africa, was probably the first Christian Church leader to use the term Trinity. The term is now used throughout the Christian Church as an attempt to express in human language the Biblical witness that there is only one God whose very essence is redemptive love. The concept of Trinity was not intended to convey that there are three gods. Never! It is an attempt to express in a simple, but profound way, that there is one true God only Who has revealed Himself by what He has done as Creator, Saviour and Spirit; this one, true, eternal God is love. He overflows with love and gives Himself in self-giving love for mankind.

### God is a mystery

It is impossible to adequately express the mystery of God as Trinity. All examples of what we mean do not seem quite right. Nevertheless, Christian witness needs to try to interpret the mystery of God as Creator, Saviour and Spirit. Some people use the analogy of a person who is: mind, body, spirit. These three dimensions of the person are a perfect unity. You are one person. Your mind, body, and spirit are united in you, yet these three qualities of your personhood are expressed in different ways. You make things with your hands. You think through problems with your mind. Your spirit is expressed through your personality. These three dimensions of your selfhood are the one person who you are.

Christians recognize that it is unwise to attempt to explain God.

We always need to remember that no analogy concerning God is ever exactly right. No one has seen God. He must remain a mystery. Our attempts to explain God are never adequate. The term Trinity is an example of the inability of human language to adequately express the mystery of God Who is one and Who is love.

## God in covenant

However, although God is a mystery, He is not unknown. The Biblical witness is that God has chosen to make Himself known to us. We have already noted that God has revealed Himself through His acts in history, and especially through His relationship with the Covenant People of Faith. It is in covenant* with God that we are able to experience His redemptive love most perfectly.

God's covenant relationship with man began at the Garden of Eden when He entered into a covenant with Adam and Eve. He commanded them to till the garden, to care for it, and to have children. Adam and Eve broke that first covenant between God and man (Genesis 1:28; 3:24). Thereafter the Biblical account reveals repeated initiatives by God to renew a covenant with mankind: Noah, Abraham, Isaac, Jacob, Moses, David and others were invited by God to participate in a covenant relationship with Him.

God's covenant initiative at the time of the Prophet Moses is particularly significant. In the Book of Exodus of the Torah in the Bible we read that the Hebrew people who were descendants of Abraham had become slaves of Pharaoh. God appeared to the Prophet Moses in the burning bush and commanded Him to deliver the Hebrews from bondage under Pharaoh. The Prophet Moses was hesitant. He feared that he would be inadequate. Finally he asked God: 'What is Your name?' God answered, 'I AM Who I AM. Say to the people I AM has sent me to you' (Exodus 3:13–15).

Moses obeyed God and became the leader of the Hebrew people, as God delivered them from horrible slavery under Pharaoh. The story is wonderfully described in Exodus.

What is the significance of the new name which God revealed to the Prophet Moses at the burning bush? God had revealed

---

*Covenant is a solemn agreement between two or more people which should never be broken. In the Bible we learn that God invites people to enter into a covenant of blessing with Himself.

Himself to the Prophet Abraham as Elohim or Allah, which is translated God Almighty.* That is the name for God used by Abraham, but to Moses, the great prophet of the Torah, God reveals Himself as I AM (Exodus 6:2,3). The Hebrew term for I AM is Yahweh. What is the significance of God as Yahweh?

God as Yahweh reveals Himself as the One Who encounters or meets people redemptively. He invites people to participate in a saving covenant relationship with Himself. He is the Covenant God. After the deliverance from slavery under Pharaoh, Yahweh God Himself met the entire Hebrew nation at Mount Sinai in the desert. The Torah describes how Yahweh met them in the thunders, lightenings, thick clouds, fire, smoke, earth quake, and trumpet blast. The people feared and trembled before the power and holiness of Yahweh God. God spoke from the mountain giving them the ten commandments, which are a marvellous guide to right and joyous living. He also invited the people to become his Covenant People. He promised that if they responded in faith and obedience to Him, He would be their Father; He would bless them, care for them, and save them. This is God as Yahweh; He is the covenant God (Exodus 19:16–20:26).

Yahweh is not far off and unknown. He is not indifferent to our need. He is grieved by our sin and rebellion. He desires to save us, to forgive our sin, to bless us with His love and grace. That is why Yahweh desires a covenant relationship with people. Because Yahweh is love, He Himself takes an initiative to enter into a covenant with people. He reveals Himself to us as the One Who encounters us with His command and invitation to become His covenant people. The Christian Church today is people who have responded to God's invitation to become His Covenant People.

In a covenant relationship with Yahweh God, we learn that He is righteous, He is love, He is just, He is holy, He can never accept that which is evil or sinful. It is because He loves us and desires to save us from evil that Yahweh God invites us into a covenant relationship with Himself. We learn to know God when we respond to His covenant invitation in faith and repentance.

The witness of the Bible and of the Christian Church is that God Who is love has chosen to invite all mankind into a covenant relationship with Himself, and that as we respond in faith to God, we learn to know Him as our loving heavenly Father Who saves us and blesses us.

---

*Elohim and Allah derive from the same Semitic root: El.

## A MUSLIM RESPONSE

When Christians and Muslims talk about God, they are talking about the same God, although their witnessing concerning God may be rather different. When they speak of God, Allah, Yahweh or Elohim, they mean the God Who is the Only One, the Creator, the Loving, the Just, the Holy, the Merciful, the Living and Eternal, the Wise and Knowing. Nevertheless, the Christian witness emphasizes the self disclosure of God (hence the 'Trinity'), while in Islam it is the will and guidance of God which is revealed.

The role of the prophet in Islam and Jesus Christ in Christianity is different, but at the same time, as messengers of the one true God, they have many things in common. The Christian witness that the most dramatic and definitive act of God in human history is the coming of the Messiah, Jesus Christ, is quite different from the Muslim view which believes deeply that the Divine Being is God Himself, not as He is incarnated in history. God, according to Muslim witness, is absolute and transcendent.

The Christian witness of God as 'Father' is also quite different from the Muslim witness. According to the true teachings of Islam, God is not to be conceived in an anthropomorphic way. He is united in design and existence. He is above all other attributes. Since He is one and the only One, a Muslim cannot invoke Him in the name of the Father, Son, or Holy Spirit. All the Divine attributes are well embedded in His Perfect Unity.

## A CHRISTIAN CLARIFICATION

When Christians refer to God as 'Father' they should not envisage God anthropomorphically. Christians share with Muslims the prohibition against conceiving of God in the form of an image. God as 'Father' refers, rather, to a relationship. God as 'Father' and mankind as sons and daughters of the heavenly Father is, from a Christian perspective, a description of covenant and fellowship relationship between God and man.

*'The earth is the Lord's and the fulness of thereof, the World and those who dwell therein'* (Psalm 24:1).

# *14.* The Creation

## THE CHRISTIAN VIEW

'In the beginning God created the heavens and the earth' (Genesis 1:1). That is the first sentence in the Bible, the first verse of the Torah of the Prophet Moses.

The Christian view of nature is based on the Biblical witness concerning creation, which is recorded in Genesis chapters one, two, and three and which is also affirmed throughout the Bible. These first chapters of the Torah give the basic framework for all that is said thereafter concerning nature. Consequently we shall rely mostly on the first three chapters of Genesis for our discussion of the Christian view of nature.

### Creation and development

There are four aspects of the creation story upon which we will comment.

*First*, we read that God is the Creator. This is profound. It means that the universe belongs to God. He formed it and He cares for it. We live on God's earth. Because He is continually concerned about the earth which He created, we are invited to pray to Him, when, for example, the rains do not fall, and work with Him when they do fall. He has created, and also cares for and preserves that which He has formed. Theologians speak of God's immanence when they consider His presence and His care for creation.

As Creator, God is other than the earth. If there were no universe, God would still be present. No part of the universe or the earth is in any sense deity. Some people think that trees are deity; they worship trees. Many peoples think that mountains are deity; they pray to the mountains. Some people worship certain animals. This is not Biblical. The Bible insists that nature is in no sense whatsoever deity. This is why many of the Hebrew prophets preached against the practice of worshipping on the 'top of every green hill.' People associated hills with deity; they thought that on the hills they were especially in contact with God or the gods. The prophets declared that this is wrong. God, Who created the universe, cannot be associated with anything that He has made because He is other than creation. Theologians call this 'otherness' of God, transcendence. God, as the Creator is both immanent and transcendent.

*Second*, although God is other than His creation, it is a good creation. In Genesis chapter one we read that after each of the six steps of creation, God said, 'It was good'. After creating man God said, 'It was very good' (Genesis 1:31). The earth is good!

Some philosophers, such as the ancient Greeks or some modern eastern teachers, believe that the material earth is not good. Only spirit is good. This is not the Biblical view. The witness of the Bible is that the earth with man on it is 'very good'. It is to be enjoyed. The sunrise and the sunset, the falling rain and the times of drought, the trees and plants and grasses, the changing seasons, the stars, moon and sun, the quiet movement of the wind, the fertile soil and the desert sands, all are good. God intends for us to enjoy His creation and give thanks for it. We read in the Scriptures that God '. . . richly furnishes us with everything to enjoy' (1 Timothy 6:17).

*Third*, the earth is understandable. Genesis chapter one describes an orderly progression in creation. God created in logical step-by-step manner: light, sky and earth, dry land and sea, plant life, the cycle of the day, night, and year with the various functions of the sun, moon and stars, sea life and birds, all forms of land animals, and finally man. This progression is described in a six-step development; each of the six days of creation was a preparation for the next phase. These six creation days are signs of the orderliness of creation. It is an orderly and understandable universe.

We have observed three basic facts concerning the Christian view of nature: first, God is other than the creation; second, it is a good creation; third, it is an orderly and understandable creation.

Our *fourth* observation concerns the role of man in creation. God placed Adam and Eve in this wonderful earth. He placed them in the Garden of Eden, and He gave them the privilege of enjoying that Garden. He said, 'Behold I have given you every plant yielding seed which is upon the face of all the earth, and every tree with seed in its fruit; you shall have them for food' (Genesis 1:29). Adam and Eve also had specific responsibilities given to them by God! They were to 'subdue' the earth and have 'dominion' over it (Genesis 1:28). They were certainly expected to do much more than only sleep and eat!

Adam and Eve were given specific commands by God. First, they were to have children; they were to fill the earth with people (Genesis 1:28). Second, they were to have dominion over the earth and to subdue it (Genesis 1:28). Third, man was to till the earth and keep the Garden (Genesis 2:15). Fourth, man was to name the animals (Genesis 2:19). And fifth, they were forbidden to eat of the tree of the knowledge of good and evil (Genesis 2:16,17). These commands are significant. They reveal to us God's intention for nature.

All of God's commands to Adam and Eve are secular, that is they concern what man is to do with the earth on which he lives. The commands show us that people should use the earth for the good of mankind. They also suggest that God expects Adam and Eve to make the good earth, which God has created, better. Note that Genesis never suggests that God created a perfect earth. The earth was 'good'. However, when man was created, God then said that it was 'very good.'

Before man was created the earth was good; after the creation of man it was very good. This suggests two things:

1. The creation of man contributes to making the earth become better than it was before man was created.
2. The 'good' or 'very good' earth was not perfect. There is the possibility of making the earth become better.

In other words, the creation of Adam and Eve *and* God's secular commands to them relate directly to making the earth become a better place. God invites man to participate with Him in caring for the earth and making it become better.

In modern terms we would say that God has commanded man to participate in 'development' and 'progress'. Learning better farming methods, building highways and factories and cities, discovering the causes of disease and using modern medicines to help cope with illnesses, controlling the size of the family so that we can give our children a fair chance to go to school and provide sufficient food for them to live healthy lives, mining the coal and ores in the ground, seeking for oil in the sea and in the deserts, raising better quality goats or camels—these are all examples of people fulfilling God's command to Adam and Eve to subdue the earth, to till the earth, to trim the Garden, in brief to use the earth for the good of man and to make it into a better place in which to live.

These concepts of development, progress, or having dominion over nature are based on the four theological legs of the creation story:

1. God is other than nature.
2. Nature is understandable.
3. Nature is good.
4. Man is to subdue nature.

These principles are the four foundation stones of the Christian approach to development. Because God is other than nature, we do not fear that a god will jump out of a tree and bite us when we chop the tree down, or that a deity will strike us with plague when we dynamite the granite rocks from a hillside. Because nature has been formed in a rational manner by God Who is reliable and trustworthy, we are confident that we can understand to some extent the mysteries of how God put nature together. Scientific investigation, which studies the laws of nature, is one way in which people can obey the command of God to subdue and have dominion over nature. Because nature is good and man has been commanded by God to subdue the earth, we experience great joy in understanding nature and in using it for the benefit of man. These are the basic building blocks of the Christian approach to technology and economic development.

## Selfishness and pride

Nevertheless, the Christian cannot stop there. The Bible also has a sober note, a serious warning. Adam and Eve were also commanded not to eat of the tree of the knowledge of good and evil. That tree which was in the middle of the Garden of Eden is a sign of the possibility of using nature irresponsibly, that is using the gifts of God selfishly, proudly, and without any sense of responsibility to God or to our fellowmen.

There are many modern examples of the tree in the garden. Perhaps a farmer plows land which is on a hillside. When the rains come, there is danger of the soil washing away. The farmer might say that since the land belongs to him, it doesn't matter what happens to his soil; he will farm just as he wants; he will not plow or plant in a manner which saves the soil from erosion. Consequently, after twenty years the soil has been washed away and his farm has become useless. His children cannot use the land, because he farmed irresponsibly and selfishly. He acted in a proud and independent way, and consequently his farm is spoiled and he and his children have become poor.

The tree of the knowledge of good and evil is a sign from God that although we are given the earth to subdue, we must live with humility. We dare not become selfish and proud and use nature in a destructive manner. We must not use all the fruit of the Garden for ourselves. Others also must share with us in the good gifts of nature.

The tree is also a sign that we need to recognize God in all our efforts in development. The earth belongs to God, not to us. God has given us the earth to subdue it for the good of mankind, but we always need to recognize that the earth is a wonderful gift from God. We need to use this good earth as faithful stewards. We need to respect God's negative commands as well as his affirmative commands. Although He has commanded us to subdue the earth, we need to remember also that He has commanded Adam and Eve not to eat from that one tree. That tree is a sign that we need to always recognize our dependence on God, and never attempt to live independently of Him.

Nevertheless, Adam and Eve did disobey God. They took the fruit from the tree of the knowledge of good and evil. By taking that fruit they declared their independence from God. They were saying that they wanted to be like God. They wanted to use all the fruit of nature selfishly and independently of God (Genesis 3:1–7).

Because Adam and Eve rebelled against God, nature became less good than it had been. In fact God 'cursed' the ground (Genesis 3:14–24). Now the ground will produce thorns and thistles. Work, which should be a blessing, will become a drudgery. From the 'sweat of your brow', you will make a living from the earth. The work of subduing the earth became much more difficult because man had turned away from God!

In the Bible, natural calamities such as drought are interpreted many times as being a form of punishment or reminder from God that we need to depend on Him, and give thanks to Him, for all the good gifts of nature. Although modern man has made great scientific strides, we are always reminded through natural calamities that we are not in ultimate control of nature. God is Lord of nature. Our capability of controlling and using nature for the good of man is dependent on God. Although we are commanded by God to commit ourselves to economic and technological development, we need to recognize that pride and selfishness distorts and destroys. Whenever we live independently of God, our achievements become curses rather than blessings.

In summary, we have learned that Christians believe that the earth is God's good gift to mankind. People are commanded by God to use the earth responsibily for the joy and well-being of mankind, but our selfishness and pride distort and destroy true and joyous development of the earth.

## A MUSLIM RESPONSE

Muslims, like Christians, do witness that God is the Creator. As Creator, He is other than creation. He is not nature; He is above and beyond His creation (transcendent). Muslims believe that God's creation is perfect.

Muslims also believe that Adam was the first man to be created and God sent him to earth to be His vicegerent. A spouse Hauwa (Eve) was created for Adam out of his own rib to give him comfort. Before Adam and Hauwa were sent down to earth, Allah ordered them to live in the Heavenly Garden (Paradise) and eat freely of all fruits of the garden. They were, however, prohibited to approach the forbidden tree.* Satan lured and tempted them into eating the fruit of the forbidden tree.

Therefore, Allah expelled them from the Garden. God sent them down to earth when they were given the honourable position of vicegerent of God on earth. 'Get ye down, (all ye people) with enemity between yourselves. On earth will be your dwelling place and your means of livelihood for a time' (Qur'an 2:36). From this verse we can say that the Muslims witness, unlike that of Christians, is that the 'Garden of Eden' given to Adam and Eve was not on earth.

Muslims, similarly, do not contribute to the Christian view that God in fact 'cursed' the ground (Genesis 3:14–24). All that God tells man in relation to the ground after the descent of Adam to earth is as quoted: **'Therein Ye shall live and therein Ye shall die, and therein Ye shall be brought forth' (Qur'an 7:25).**

---

*This tree is not specified in the Qur'an and is nameless. Some commentators think it was a tree of evil.

## A CHRISTIAN CLARIFICATION

The Biblical reference to the ground being 'cursed' following the fall of man is primarily a description of broken and inappropriate relationships between man and nature. It is noteworthy that the text referred to says that the ground is cursed 'because of you' (Genesis 3:17). Certainly the exploitative and selfish use of nature by man is a curse on nature. Elsewhere, the Bible dramatically describes nature as 'groaning' until man is fully redeemed from his sinfulness (Romans 8:19–23).

*'Thou hast crowned [man and woman] with glory and honour'* (Hebrews 2:7b).

# 15. Adam and Eve

## THE CHRISTIAN BELIEF

> Then God said, 'Let us make man in our image, after our likeness; and let them have dominion over the fish of the sea, and over the birds of the air, and over the cattle, and over all the earth, and over every creeping thing that creeps upon the earth.' So God created man in His own image, in the image of God He created him; male and female He created them. And God blessed them, . . . (Genesis 1:26, 27).

In the next chapter we read that the Lord God breathed into man '. . .the breath of life, and man became a living being' (Genesis 2:7).

### The image and likeness of God

These are the first references to man in the Bible; this is the witness of the first two chapters of the Torah of the Prophet Moses. People are created in the image and likeness of God!
Man is a living soul! God breathed into man the breath of life! What does this mean?

Man as a living soul created in the image of God does *not* mean that man looks like God, or that God is anthropomorphic. The meaning of man created in the likeness of God does not suggest any kind of physical likeness between God and man. Obviously not! Rather it suggests a deep spiritual reality. It shows that man is capable of a profound convenant relationship with God.

We need to hear the witness of the Bible as a whole in order to comprehend the reality of man created in the image and likeness of God. Much of the rest of the Bible is really a further development of the deep inner meaning of man created in the image and likeness of God, of man as a living soul, who has received the breath of life from God. We can only touch the surface in this chapter, but we shall attempt to mention some of the more important dimensions to this Biblical teaching concerning man created in the likeness of God.

First, note that both the man and the woman are created in the image and likeness of God (Genesis 1:27). Woman is not less important than the man. Both are equally important and equally human. Mankind, both male and female, are in the likeness of God.

Second, our God-likeness means that we can begin to understand creation. In the last chapter we learned that man is commanded by God to have dominion over the earth. We noticed that this includes the ability to study and understand the marvelous laws of nature. It is amazing that the human mind can begin to comprehend the complexity of the laws of genetics and heredity, or that man can use the laws of gravity, thrust, and inertia so effectively that he is able to travel to the moon. These are complex achievements. Equally significant is our ability to build homes in which to live, to plant gardens for food, or herd our cattle taking them to the right kind of pastures so that they will give the maximum amount of milk. Man in the likeness of God, not only understands aspects of God's wonderful creation, but he also knows how to use that creation to build a better life for himself.

Third, we are cultural beings. Animals do not create culture. As mentioned, animals operate by instinct or learned behaviour, but people create cultures, which vary greatly. All dogs around the world bark in much the same manner, but human languages have immense diversity. Language is one significant aspect of culture; it is a creation of human society. Similarly people live in a vast variety of houses, they create a tremendous diversity of clothing, and cook thousands of different foods. Nature shows us that God also creates enormous variety! Notice, for example, that every human being is different. Our cultural creativity is a dimension of our God-likeness.

Fourth, we know right from wrong. Man is a moral being; he does not operate primarily by instinct like the animals do. The sense of right and wrong is embedded deeply in the conscience of man. Even though human cultures vary greatly, everywhere there is a deep sense of right and wrong. For example, although specific cultural expressions are different, people everywhere seem to sense that it is not right to kill a fellow human being. This moral consciousness is a very significant aspect of our being created in the image of God.

Fifth, man senses that he should grow to become a better person. People in all cultures seem to have an awareness that they are not as good, or shall we say human, as they should be. This is the witness of our God-likeness within our conscience. It is a persistent voice in the conscience that we should become better people, that we do not always do what we know we should do, that we really should be more kind, brave, true, reliable, more God-like. Conscience, that voice which calls us to do better, is the stamp of the image of God deep within our spirits. It is a call to grow, to become a better person.

Sixth, human societies everywhere have a sense that man is immortal. We know that when we die, that is not the end to our personal existence. We sense that there is life beyond the grave. This is a significant aspect of our being created in the image of God. God is eternal. In a similar manner God has graciously determined that we shall not vanish when our bodies die. God has determined that man, whom He has created in His own image and likeness, shall experience eternity and immortality. We shall say more about this in a later chapter.

Seventh, the image of God means that we can have fellowship with our fellow human beings and with God. Speech is important in the experience of fellowship; it is evidence that we are personal, and that we long to relate to others in a deep and personal way. God also desires to have fellowship with us. God cannot have fellowship with animals because they are not personal; they are not created in the image of God. But man is different. Man is a fellowship creature. He is personal. He is created in the image and likeness of God.

The first chapters of Genesis describe Adam and Eve as having blessed fellowship with God. God spoke with them. He conversed with them in the cool of the evening. This is God's intention for man. He desires to relate to man in joyous and personal fellowship. That is why God invites man into a covenant relationship. The covenant between God and man is a fellowship relationship which the Bible describes as being similar to that between a father and his children. In fact, that is the central aspect of being created in the image and likeness of God: we are His beloved children; God is our heavenly Father (Deuteronomy 32:6, Psalm 103:13, Jeremiah 31:9, Romans 8:14–17).

The Bible teaches that man finds his truest humanity in a deep and meaningful covenant relationship with God. We are truly human when we live in a right and joyous relationship with God. When our loyalty and love for God is eroded, when we turn away from God and devote our lives to false gods, when we ourselves begin to live independently of God, then our humanity is distorted and spoiled.

Marriage is a sign of covenant fellowship with God. In Genesis chapter two we read that after God had created Eve out of a rib in Adam's side, Adam joyously accepted her as his wife and said,

> This at last is bone of my bone and flesh of my flesh; she shall be called woman because she was taken out of man.

The account goes on to say,

> Therefore a man leaves his father and his mother and cleaves to his wife, and they become one flesh. And the man and his wife were both naked, and were not ashamed (Genesis 2:23–25).

It is for this reason that Christians do not accept polygamy as God's ideal form of marriage. In this first account of marriage in the Bible, we read that in marriage the man and the woman become one flesh. When a man has more than one wife, his loyalties are divided between several women. Divided loyalty distorts and spoils the 'one flesh' unity which God intends between a man and a woman.

In much the same manner, when we give our ultimate loyalty to any authority other than God, our relationship to God is then distorted and spoiled. True fellowship with God involves total commitment to Him, just as true fellowship in marriage demands total and exclusive commitment to one's partner in marriage (Hosea 2:14–3:5).

## The sin of humanity

Tragically, Adam and Eve did not continue to give God their first loyalty. They turned away from God. They listened to the voice of the serpent, who is a sign of Satan, and they took and ate fruit from the tree of the knowledge of good and evil, which God had strictly forbidden. By eating that fruit, Adam and Eve declared their independence from God. The Bible says they took the fruit because they wanted to be 'like God'. This is rebellion. It is a declaration of pride and selfishness (Genesis 3:1-7).

The witness of the Bible is that this act of rebellion by our first parents has seriously and tragically distorted and spoiled man as created in the image of God. Although hints of the image of God remain, mankind has collectively turned away from God and sinfulness pervades us individually and collectively. Our sinfulness is a cancer which destroys (Romans 3:23).

Mankind's rebellion against God begins right at the origin of human history. Adam and Eve, the first parents of all mankind, turned away from God; they broke God's wonderful covenant with them. That very evening, after taking the fruit from the tree, God appeared in the Garden to speak with Adam and Eve, but they were hiding behind the bushes, afraid and ashamed. God called, 'Adam, where are you?' Adam replied, 'I heard the sound of Thee in the garden, and I was afraid, because I was naked; and I hid myself' (Genesis 3:9, 10).

God did not leave Adam and Eve. Rather Adam and Eve hid from God. God did not break His covenant with them. It was they who broke their covenant with God.

God never leaves us. Because He is love, He always seeks for us and invites us to become His covenant people. It is we ourselves who turn away from Him and refuse to accept His invitation to become His people. This is the story of human history! The story of mankind rejecting God, turning away from Him, neglecting His wonderful invitation to become part of His covenant community of faith.

All of this gives two pictures of mankind. On the one hand we are created in the image of God and are invited to participate in a marvellous covenant fellowship with God. On the other hand we have turned away from God. The human race as a whole is in rebellion against God. We more easily do what is evil than what is good.

In the next chapter we shall say more about the Christian understanding of evil and the way in which it pervades human society. Then we shall also look at the Biblical witness concerning God's wonderful plan to save mankind from sin, and the way in which God graciously attempts to recreate the image of God within us, which has been spoiled by our turning away from our heavenly Father.

## A MUSLIM RESPONSE

The Christian witness, that man is created in the 'image and likeness of God', is not the same as the Muslim witness. Although God breathed into man His spirit, as both Christians and Muslims believe, for Islam the only Divine quality that was entrusted to man as a result of God's breath was the faculty of knowledge, will, and power of action. If man uses these Divine qualities rightly in understanding God and following His law strictly, then he has nothing to fear in the present or the future, and no sorrow for the past.

Islam further teaches that man is not only made in the best form of all creation, but has been made God's *khalifa* (vicegerent) on earth. This dignity is the natural right of both male and female, and all people regardless of race, language, or culture. The dignity of man is the supreme privilege of being the servants or slaves of Allah. It is in total submission to the will of Allah that the dignity of man is most fully evident. Allah says: 'Surely We created man of the best stature, then we reduced him to the lowest of the low, save those who believe and do good works and theirs is a reward unfailing' (Qur'an 95:4-6).

The Christian witness that the rebellion by our first parents has tragically distorted man, and that sinfulness pervades us individually and collectively, is very much contrary to Islamic witness. Islam teaches that the first phase of life on earth did not begin in sin and rebellion against Allah. Although Adam disobeyed Allah, he repented and was forgiven and even given guidance for mankind. Man is not born a sinner and the doctrine of the sinfulness of man has no basis in Islam.

However, despite a different conception of man in Christianity and Islam, they both believe that man needs revelation. In Islam the revelation consists of Divine guidance for man, whereas in Christianity, the central concern of revelation is redemption from sin.

*'The heart is deceitful above all things, and desperately corrupt; who can understand it?' (Jeremiah 17:9).*

# 16. Sin and Evil

## THE CHRISTIAN VIEW

Evil does not come from God, Who is the righteous Creator. Evil does not spring naturally out of the good earth which God has created. It has nothing to do with the material aspects of creation, as the ancient Greek philosophers believed. They thought that spirit is good, and material evil. For them evil was bound up in the material or body-like aspects of creation. The Bible rejects all such notions of the origin of evil. Furthermore, evil is not caused by ignorance. Knowledge in itself is not necessarily good, nor is ignorance necessarily bad. Neither God nor His good creation is the cause of evil.

According to the Bible, we become evil when we turn away from God. Before Adam and Eve sinned, they did not experience evil, but when they took the fruit from the tree of the knowledge of good and evil, they immediately began to experience that something was seriously wrong within themselves, in their relationships to each other, in their relationship to God, and to the good earth which God had created for them to enjoy.

In the last chapter, we mentioned that taking the fruit from the tree of the knowledge of good and evil was a declaration of independence from God. It was an expression of pride; they wanted to be 'like God' (Genesis 3:4). It was also a selfish act; they desired all the fruit of the Garden for themselves (Genesis 3:6). It was disobedience. God had commanded them not to eat of that one tree (Genesis 3:11).

It was Adam and Eve themselves who decided to turn away from God (Genesis 3:1-7). It is true that Satan was present in the form of a serpent. Satan tempted them to eat the fruit, but he was not the central figure in the drama. It is the man and woman who were at the centre of the rebellion against God. It is they who listened to the serpent's temptation and took the fruit. They reached out their own hands to take the fruit from the tree. It was their personal decision to sin against God.

Sin enters the world through the misuse of human freedom. All of us participate in the sin of mankind; all of us have misused our freedom. The Bible says, 'All we like sheep have gone astray; we have turned every one to his own way . . .' (Isaiah 53:6a). We are personally and collectively responsible.

At the beginning of human history, mankind turned away from God. We should not blame Adam and Eve or our own parents for our sinfulness. All of us have personally experienced the meaning of rebellion against God. When we reflect on the story of Adam and Eve, we are really reflecting on our own personal story as well. Each of us has fallen '. . . short of the glory of God' (Romans 3:23). The tragic consequences of this rebellion are described in Genesis chapters three and four. The story of Adam and Eve is the story of each of us. It is the story of history, the story of humanity. Here are some of the consequences of sin, for Adam and Eve and for each of us.

First, Adam and Eve became ashamed of themselves (Genesis 3:7). Before they turned against God, they were not ashamed in each other's presence. They did not wear clothing. They had a beautiful and shameless relationship with each other, but after they disobeyed God, they began to try to hide themselves. They sewed fig leaves together as aprons to cover themselves. They hid behind the bushes in the Garden. They were ashamed. We also try to cover our true selves with the fashionable clothing we wear or the smiles on our faces. We try to pretend that we are different from what we really are. We are ashamed of our true self, and so we pretend. We become insincere. Shame, pretence, and insincerity is a consequence of our sin. This is hypocrisy!

Second, Adam and Eve were afraid. They hid behind the bushes in the Garden. They were afraid of each other, and they were also afraid of God. When God appeared in the Garden as usual to have fellowship with the man and the woman, they were hiding from God. They were crouching behind the bushes hoping that God could not find them there. God called, 'Where are you?'

Adam answered, 'I heard the sound of Thee in the garden, and I was afraid, because I was naked, and I hid myself' (Genesis 3:9,10).

Man and woman afraid of God! Hiding behind the bushes! Man created in the image of God, man whose greatest joy should be right and joyous fellowship with the Creator, this man is hiding from God His loving heavenly Father. Man has separated himself from God, he has turned away from God, he is hiding behind the bushes. Adam and Eve, sons and daughters of God, have alienated themselves from their heavenly Father. Instead of loving God, they feared Him! Instead of having fellowship with God, they ran to hide from God!

Third, Adam and Eve did not accept blame for what they had done; they made excuses for their sin.

God asked Adam, 'Have you eaten of the tree which I commanded you not to eat?'

Adam answered, 'The woman whom Thou gavest to be with me, she gave me fruit of the tree, and I ate.'

Then Eve said, 'The serpent beguiled me, and I ate' (Genesis 3:12,13).

Adam blamed Eve for his sin. Indirectly he also blamed God. He said that it is the woman God gave him who caused him to sin. Eve, of course, blamed Satan. Neither accepted any personal blame. They made excuses for their sin.

We are like that. When we know that we have done wrong, we blame others. Sometimes we blame God for our sin. Perhaps we say, because God is sovereign and all powerful, then sin is really the fault of God. Or we may think that God should not have permitted a temptation to come into our lives. We might even become bitter against God for a certain temptation or misfortune which we experience. More often we blame Satan for our sin: 'He is the one who caused us to sin', we say. Frequently we blame our parents or our brothers and sisters for our failure. This common human experience of blaming others for the evil that we do is called the psycho-projection of guilt by modern psychologists. We wrongly blame others for the evil which we do.

Fourth, the marriage relationship was spoiled. Before they sinned, Adam and his wife had a beautiful relationship, but after they sinned, they began to hide their true selves from each other. We also read that Adam began to dominate his wife, and she submitted to him (Genesis 3:16). This kind of relationship in marriage is a form of exploitation. The husband rules, and the wife submits. Because of man's rebellion against God, sex became exploitative. Women dress and act in ways that attract men. Men, on the other hand, are aggressive and try to get women to submit to them in marriage, and even outside of marriage.

Even the experience of childbirth became painful (Genesis 3:16). Children should be a great blessing in any home, but our sinfulness brings pain into the experience of having children.

Children are born through pain; they also cause their parents pain through disobedience and rebellion.

Fifth, work became a drudgery for mankind (Genesis 3:17–19). Before man turned away from God, work was a blessing; it was central to the covenant God made with Adam and Eve. They were commanded to work to make the earth better, but after they rebelled against God their relationship to nature became difficult. Man began to exploit nature and the earth groaned under the exploitation. The ground was cursed because of man. Thistles began to grow on the land which man cultivated for his crops. Man became unkind to nature, and similarly nature became unkind to him. Man began to struggle and fight with nature; 'in the sweat of (his) face', he needed to work for his living.

Sixth, death came. God is the Life-Giver. We experience life when we live in a joyous relationship with God, Who is the eternal giver of life. When Adam and Eve turned away from God, when they declared their independence from God, they were really declaring independence from the Life-Giver. By turning away from God, they were actually turning towards death. We die because we live in rebellion against God. The Bible says, 'the wages of sin is death' (Romans 6:23).

Death, in the Biblical sense, is far more serious than biological death. Obviously, man who has the body of a creature does experience bodily death. Biological death might be an aspect of the consequence of sin, but it is certainly not the central meaning of death as a result of turning away from God. The deeper meaning of death is the tragic spoiling of man created in the image of God. Our lives should reflect the glory and righteousness of God. Instead we are selfish and proud. Our humanity is spoiled. We hate instead of love. We exploit instead of share. We become bitter instead of forgiving. We become small instead of great. We become like Satan rather than like God. We are deceitful rather than truthful. We go further and further away from God; we experience death throughout our being. Death is eternal separation from God! Separation from God is the ultimate evil. Separation from God is death.

Seventh, death spreads and poisons the whole human family and all our relationships. In the family of Adam and Eve, death reigned. Cain, the eldest son, murdered Abel, the second born (Genesis 4:1–16). Cain murdered his brother because he was jealous of him. The first human family experienced murder. The elder son killed his younger brother!

This murder in the first human family is a sign that sin has spread beyond Adam and Eve. Their children also experienced rebellion against God. In fact, rebellion against God has spread throughout the human race. Everyone, everywhere shares in the rebellion against God. The Bible says, 'None is righteous, no, not one' (Romans 3:10). Again we read, 'In Adam all die...' (1 Corinthians 15:22). The Prophet Isaiah writes, 'All we like sheep have gone astray! we have turned everyone to his own way;...' (Isaiah 53:6). Each of us individually, as well as all of human society, shares in the experience of rebellion against God and death. Our common humanity is tragically spoiled. Man as son of God, created in the image of God, has turned against God; he is sinful rather than righteous; he dies rather than lives.

Our sin is rebellion. It is more than the wrong acts which we sometimes do. It is we ourselves who are sinful. It is our hearts which are evil. The Bible says, 'The heart is deceitful above all things and desperately corrupt; who can understand it' (Jeremiah 17:9). The wrong things which we do are a consequence of our evil hearts. We ourselves are sinful. That is why we do wrong.

The Bible describes the astonishing manner in which man throughout history has experienced sin and death. Even the Priest Aaron helped the people of the covenant form a golden calf which they worshipped (Exodus 32)! And the Prophet David committed adultery and arranged for the murder of the good husband of the woman with whom he had sinned (2 Samuel 11). Even the prophets experience sin! The Bible is absolutely honest. Adam, Noah, Abraham, Moses, Aaron, David, all these men of God described in the Bible experienced failure and sin. The Bible reveals that often those who seem to be righteous are really hypocrites and insincere. The Bible says, 'All have sinned!'

History is also evidence of the sinfulness of man. All our history books from every culture and civilization are the stories of wars. History is the story of death: man killing man; destruction of the good things which man has built; the rise and fall of empires; the death of civilization; the death of empires; the death of people through wars and conflict. Humanity has fallen into death. We have turned away from God. Death is our common experience.

Rebellion against God extends beyond the human family into the world of spirits and angels. These spiritual beings are also personal and have free will. They can turn against God if they wish. Satan is an angel who rebelled. He became proud and turned against God (Isaiah 14:12–14). Other angels followed his example. These evil angels obey the command of Satan who is called '. . . the prince of the power of the air, the spirit. . . of disobedience' (Ephesians 2:2). Satan and the evil angels and spirits which he leads are in total rebellion against God. They seek to destroy all that is good. The Bible calls these evil forces '. . . the spiritual hosts of wickedness in heavenly places' (Ephesians 6:12). These evil spiritual powers are death oriented. They attempt to bind people and societies in death.

Whether evil comes through spiritual and unseen powers or through human sinfulness, it is always the consequence of rebellion against God. Who is the righteous Life-Giver. All forms of rebellion against God are evil. To live in a right and joyous relationship with God is always good, but mankind has disobeyed God. For this reason we experience death.

So our problem is this: How can we be saved from death? How can we who have turned away from God begin to experience again the joy of life? How can the image of God be recreated which has been spoiled through rebellion? The Bible is about the answer to those questions.


## A MUSLIM RESPONSE

While Muslims agree with the Christian witness that Adam and Eve disobeyed God by eating the fruit of the forbidden tree, the course of events that followed the incident is related differently by the two faiths. According to the Christian view, when Adam and Eve took the fruit, they were declaring their independence of God and wanted to become like God.

The Muslim belief is that Adam and Eve, having realized their mistake or sin, prayed to God for forgiveness, and they were pardoned. Adam was also made the first messenger of God on earth. The Christian witness minimizes the role of Satan and apportions the blame of the rebellion on man himself. Our submission is that Satan, the power of evil, was central in the whole drama, and was very responsible for Adam's fall from the Garden.

As Muslims, we do not accuse Adam and Eve of transmitting sin and evil to the whole of mankind. The two were absolved of their sin, and their descendents were made immune from its effect. Sin is not original, hereditary, or inevitable. It is not from God. It is acquirable through choice, but also avoidable through knowledge and true guidance from God. Muslims believe that man is fundamentally a good and dignified creature. He is not a fallen being. Muslims certainly would not agree that even prophets have participated in sinfulness!

## A CHRISTIAN CLARIFICATION

While it is true that some Christian theologians have often spoken of concepts such as original sin or hereditary sinfulness, these specific terms do not adequately explain the collective and personal sinfulness of mankind of which the Bible speaks. From a Biblical perspective, it is far more important to recognize that we need redemption from our sinfulness, than it is to develop theories as to precisely how sin is or is not transmitted.

*'Thy word is a lamp to my feet and a light to my path'* (Psalm 119:105).

# 17. The Word of God

**WHAT ARE THE CHRISTIAN SCRIPTURES?**
Christians believe that the Bible is the written Word of God; it is inspired by God. The witness of the Bible concerning itself is,

> All scripture is inspired by God and is profitable for teaching, for reproof, for correction, and for training in righteousness, that the man of God may be complete, equipped for every good work (2 Timothy 3:16,17).

The word 'inspire' means to breathe. Christians believe that the Holy Scriptures have been 'breathed' by God. The thoughts of God were breathed into the holy men of God who spoke or wrote God's Word. The Bible has been inspired by God.

Divine inspiration does not mean Divine dictation. Christians do not believe that the prophets who spoke or wrote the Word of God were tubes through which God's words flowed. In all of the Biblical scriptures, the personality of the different writers is evident. The Prophet David wrote as an inspired poet; he was a poet. The Prophet Jeremiah spoke as an inspired preacher; he was a preacher. The gifts and personalities of the writers are part of the scriptural message. God's inspiring activity does not abrogate human involvement in the process; the imprint of human personality is part of the content of Biblical revelation. The Bible is the marvellous drama of God revealing Himself to man, and the inspired prophets of God expressing that revelation in human language and thought forms.

## The organization of the Bible

The Bible is divided into two major parts: The Old Testament and the New Testament. Testament means covenant or a sacred promise which should not be broken. The Old Testament, or Old Covenant, refers to the covenant which God made with the people of Israel at Mount Sinai, after He had delivered them from slavery under the Pharoah. It was at Mount Sinai that God gave the People of Israel the Ten Commandments (Exodus 20:1–17).

He invited them to become His covenant people, and promised to care for them as a father for his children. The Old Testament is the record of God's revelation of Himself and the response of the people of faith to become His covenant people.

Tragically, the people of Israel failed to trust in God as they should. Even when they were still at Mount Sinai, they began to worship a golden calf. Repeatedly they turned away from God. They were not able, and often not willing, to obey the good commands of God. They were a sinful people (Exodus 32:7-10). Slowly God led the prophets of the Old Testament to realize that the old covenant was not adequate. They came to recognize that God would make a new covenant with mankind, a covenant of power and grace which would transform the inner heart of mankind, a covenant which would recreate the image of God within man, which was spoiled so tragically through man's rebellion against God.

The Prophet Jeremiah speaks of the new covenant in this way:

> Behold, the days are coming, says the Lord, when I will make a new covenant with the house of Israel, . . .I will put My law within them, and I will write it upon their hearts; and I will be their God, and they shall be My people (Jeremiah 31:31,33).

The prophets of the Old Testament also recognized that the new covenant would be fulfilled through the Messiah. In fact, even at the time when Adam and Eve sinned, God revealed that a child born to the woman would crush the head of evil (Genesis 3:15). Although this is the first prophecy concerning the Messiah in the Bible, we find that the prophetic development throughout the Old Testament increasingly anticipated that the promises of God to mankind would be fulfilled and completed in the Messiah. He is the One through Whom God would create a new and better covenant with mankind (Isaiah 11:1-9).

The Old Testament prophesies concerning the Messiah were amazingly specific. Here are a few examples:

> He would be from King David's family (2 Samuel 7:12-13).
> He would be born of a virgin (Isaiah 7:14).
> He would be born in Bethlehem (Micah 5:2).
> He would be 'God with us' (Isaiah 7:14).
> He would not be accepted by mankind (Isaiah 53:3-9).
> He would suffer and die with the wicked (Psalm 22:16-17).

He would be buried in a rich man's grave (Isaiah 53:9).
He would rise from the dead (Psalm 16:10).

These are only a very few of the many Old Testament prophecies about the coming Messiah, all of which were perfectly fulfilled by Jesus.

The New Testament is the record of the manner in which God fulfilled the Old Testament prophecies concerning the Messiah and established the new covenant. It contains the account of the life and teachings of the Messiah, and the creation of the Church which is the new covenant community. This portion of the Bible describes the manner in which God fulfilled His promises, which were given through the prophets of the old covenant. The Old Testament anticipates the coming of the Messiah. The New Testament reveals to us that the Messiah has come.

Both the Old Testament and the New Testament are necessary for us to understand and accept God's revelation to mankind. The Old Testament is a preparation for the New Testament; the Old is a sign of the New; the New fulfills the Old. Christians accept both the Old and New Testament as God's inspired written Word.

Now we need to look more closely at the contents of these two parts of the Bible: The Old Testament and the New Testament.

## The Old Testament

The teachings and writings of about thirty prophets are included in the Old Testament. God's revelation through some of the prophets is so significant that whole sections of the Old Testament are named after particular prophets. For example, the revelation of God through the Prophet Jeremiah is recorded in the book of the Old Testament called Jeremiah. Other portions of the Old Testament mostly concern the history of the covenant people. Other parts are the songs and hymns which were chanted by the people in worship. These different types of scripture have been divided into three main divisions within the Old Testament: The Torah, the Prophets, the Writings. We will comment on each of these major parts of the Old Testament scriptures.

The Torah (*Taurat*) of the Prophet Moses is the first part of the Old Testament. It contains the first six books of the Bible: Genesis, Exodus, Leviticus, Numbers, Deuteronomy, Joshua. Moses is the great prophet of the Torah, and in fact of the entire Old Testament. In the Torah we read that God specifically commanded Moses to write the words of the covenant (Exodus 34:27–28). This is unusual. Usually in the Old Testament the prophet 'saw' or 'heard' the Word of the Lord, which he proclaimed to the people. Faithful disciples or scribes then wrote the Word of God which had been revealed through the prophet (for example, note Jeremiah 36:4). But with Moses, we read that he himself wrote portions of God's revelation with his own hand (Deuteronomy 31:9). We are confident that the Torah as a whole has come to us through the Prophet Moses and his faithful disciples, who preserved and transmitted these inspired revelations so that we can read them today. *

The second part of the Old Testament is The Writings. The Writings include books on the history of the covenant people and poetry. The history books are: Judges, Ruth, 1 and 2 Samuel, 1 and 2 Kings, 1 and 2 Chronicles, Ezra, Nehemiah, Esther. The books of poetry are: Job, Psalms, Proverbs, Song of Solomon, and Ecclesiastes. Of these five books of poetry, the best known is the Psalms. Muslims call the Psalms, the Zabur of the Prophet David. Certainly David did write many of these psalms which are beautiful hymns of praise to God for his great love and mercy to mankind.

The third portion of the Old Testament is the Prophets. These books are Isaiah, Jeremiah, Lamentations, Ezekiel, Daniel, Hosea, Joel, Amos, Obadiah, Jonah, Micah, Nahum, Habakkuk, Zephaniah, Haggai, Zechariah, Malachi. In a sense all of the writings of the Old Testament are prophetic. However, whenever the faith of the people of the covenant seemed to be in decline, God would send prophets to call the people back to Himself. All of the prophets commanded the people to repent and return to God, and the covenant which He had established with them at Mount Sinai when He revealed the Ten Commandments to them through the Prophet Moses. Yet at the same time, the prophets began to recognize that the old covenant was not good enough. They looked forward to the coming of the Messiah, whose life and teachings are recorded in the New Testament.

One of the greatest Old Testament prophets was Isaiah. This great Prophet foresaw in a marvellous way that the Messiah would come to establish a new covenant which would be a blessing to all mankind. He also prophesied that the Messiah would suffer and give His life for the sins of the people.

---

*W. F. Albright, *From the Stone Age to Christianity*, New York, Doubleday, 1957, pp.249–272.

## The New Testament

The first portion of the New Testament consists of four books which are known as the Gospel or the *Injil.* * Christians believe that the Messiah Himself is the Gospel. We shall say more about this in a later chapter, but for now it is important to recognize that the Gospel is the record of the life and teachings of Jesus the Messiah. It consists of both His life and His teachings, because He Himself is the Gospel. What the Messiah is and does are just as significant forms of revelation as what He taught and proclaimed. Consequently, the written Gospel is a presentation of the Messiah.

The Gospel, Who is the Messiah, was seen by people. Those who were the closest to the Messiah were called disciples. Some of these disciples became apostles of God. These apostles were witnesses of the Gospel. They had lived and been with the Messiah. They knew Him personally. After the death and resurrection of the Messiah, God inspired the apostles to record what they had seen and heard. The record of four of these witnesses has been written in four books. They are: Matthew, Mark, Luke, John. Each of these books is an apostolic witness concerning Jesus the Messiah, Who is the Gospel. The witness aspect of these Gospel Scriptures is beautifully affirmed in the opening verses of the Gospel as recorded by Luke:

> Inasmuch as many have undertaken to compile a narrative of the things which have been accomplished among us, just as they were delivered to us by those who from the beginning were eyewitnesses and ministers of the word, it seemed good to me also, having followed all things closely for some time past, to write an orderly account for you, most excellent Theophilus, that you may know the truth concerning the things of which you have been informed (Luke 1:1-4).

The Gospel witness has been recorded through the inspiration of God so that we 'may know the truth' (Luke 1:4).

The New Testament includes much more than the record of the life and teachings of Jesus Christ. The fifth book of the New Testament is called The Acts of the Apostles. This book is a brief history of the apostolic Church. It describes the manner in which the new

---

*Gospel is an English translation of the Greek word *euaggellion* which is commonly known as evangel. *Euaggellion* or Evangel means the Good News. The Arabic equivalent of the Evangel is *Injil.* Consequently Muslims refer to the Gospel as *Injil.* In Swahili the word *Injili* is used.

covenant community was formed, and the way in which the people of the new covenant carried forward their mission in the world, continuing the work which Jesus the Messiah had begun. A number of sermons by apostles are included. These messages reveal the basic meaning of the life, death, and resurrection of Jesus the Messiah. The Acts of the Apostles is the earliest history of the Church.

Then come the Epistles. These are letters written by apostles or apostolic men, who interpreted the meaning of the Gospel. They are: Romans, 1 and 2 Corinthians, Galatians, Ephesians, Philippians, Colossians, 1 and 2 Thessalonians, 1 and 2 Timothy, Titus, Philemon, Hebrews, James, 1 and 2, Peter, 1, 2, and 3 John, Jude, Revelation. Some of these letters were written to particular groups of Christians, giving advice and teaching concerning problems which had developed in the Church, and others were written to Church leaders.

For example, Philippians was written by the Apostle Paul to the Church in Philippi in Macedonia. The Epistle to the Hebrews describes the Messiah as the marvellous fulfillment of the Old Testament. It interprets the sacrificial offerings of animals as a sign of the sacrificial death and resurrection of Jesus the Messiah. Another letter, by James, describes the manner in which Christians should live. All these letters to churches explain Christian belief and conduct.

Other letters were written to Church leaders to guide them in the way in which they should lead the Church. For example, there are two letters written by the Apostle Paul to a young Bishop named Timothy. Another interesting little letter, called Philemon, is written to a slave master, instructing him to love his slave like a brother. Probably the master freed his slave after getting that letter from an apostle of God! The last book of the New Testament is the Revelation, which is a heavenly description of the triumph of the glorified Messiah at the end of history when God's purpose for mankind is fulfilled.

The Bible is a marvellous book. The teachings of more than thirty prophets and apostles are recorded in the Bible. The writings of the Biblical Scriptures span more than a thousand years. They were written in times of tremendous change and diversity. Yet a common thread unites all these writings: God is at work in history. His intention is to redeem and save mankind from death. His redemptive activity is fulfilled and consumated in Jesus the Messiah.

## Manuscripts and translations

For well over a thousand years, all Biblical manuscripts were copied by hand. When a manuscript is copied, there is always the possibility of variations accidentally creeping into the text because of human error. It was only in the late fifteenth century that printing began to be used for Bibles, thus eliminating the possibility of these kinds of manuscript errors. Nevertheless, Biblical scholars are concerned that the present printed texts in our possession be free of any variations from the original text. In order to do this, they compare our present printed texts with the most ancient available hand copied texts.

Biblical scholars attempt to make sure that the text of the Bible which we have in our possession today is an accurate transmission of the original. The first Old Testament was written in Hebrew and the New Testament was written in Greek. Scholars desire to know for sure that our present Hebrew and Greek texts are reliable. They use the most sophisticated textual, linguistic, and archaeological tools to accomplish their task.

In recent years several astonishing discoveries of ancient manuscripts have greatly enhanced textual studies. For example, the 1947 discovery of the Dead Sea Scrolls at Qumran near the Dead Sea has given scholars access to manuscripts of the Old Testament which date from the second century B.C. Likewise, New Testament studies have been helped by several discoveries of ancient manuscripts, one of which takes us to within one hundred years of the crucifixion of Jesus. There are now at least 5000 ancient New Testament manuscripts available for scholarly analysis. These studies of the ancient texts have greatly increased confidence in the accuracy of the Bible as we have it today. For example, scholars assure us that the possibility of any variation from the original New Testament text is now only one to a thousand! And none of the 00.1% possible variations is of any significance in terms of the message which the Bible conveys!*

The Christian concern for establishing the reliability of the Biblical texts is based on commitment to the authority of God's written Word. Respect for the authority of God's written Word springs from the pages of the Bible itself. The witness of Jesus the Messiah concerning the Old Testament Scripture is, 'For truly, I say to you, till heaven and earth pass away, not an iota, not a

---

*Sean Kealy, *The Changing Bible*, Nairobi, KUC, N.D., p.87.

dot, will pass from the law until all is accomplished' (Matthew 5:18). Even the dots and the commas were considered significant by Jesus!

One of the most severe warnings to be found in the Bible is against those who would attempt to change the inspired Word of God. In the Book of Revelation in the last chapter of the Bible we read:

> I warn everyone who hears the words of the prophecy of this book: If any one adds to them, God will add to him the plagues described in this book, and if any one takes away from the words of the book of this prophecy, God will take away his share in the tree of life and in the holy city, which are described in this book (Revelation 22:18, 19).

Although this warning is directed specifically against those who would tamper with the prophecies of the Book of Revelation, many Christians sense that is it also a general warning to all those who tamper with any part of God's written Word. Christians, who believe that the Bible is God's inspired Word, seek to make certain that the texts which have been handed on for scores of generations over many hundreds of years are accurate and reliable.

Christians believe that the Bible should be translated into the languages of people. The Biblical message is that God has chosen to reveal Himself to mankind. His revelation is understood best when it is communicated in one's own mother tongue. For this reason, as early as the third century after Christ, Christians were already at work translating the Bible from Hebrew and Greek into local languages: Syriac in Syria was probably the first, then Egyptian, Latin in North Africa, Ge'ez in Ethiopia. Today this great activity of translating the Bible into local languages is one of the most important tasks of Christian missionaries. At least some portions of the Bible have already been translated from the original Hebrew and Greek texts into 1600 languages in countries around the world. The Church desires to continue translating the Bible until every man and woman everywhere can read God's written Word in his own mother tongue.

Christians believe that the Bible is God's written Word. The Bible is the witness and record of God's actions within the history of the covenant people, and His creation of a new covenant through Jesus the Messiah. The Bible contains the inspired prophetic interpretations of God's actions.

## A MUSLIM RESPONSE

The Qur'an is very respectful of the Torah (*Taurat*), the Psalms (*Zabur*), and the Gospels (*Injil*), which form the major part of the Christian Scriptures. These scriptures are acknowledged as true Divine guidance. The prophets to whom these scriptures were revealed (Moses, David, and Jesus) are believed to be great prophets of Allah and Islam. For a Muslim to deny the prophethood of Moses (Musa), David (Daud), or Jesus (Isa) is to deny the true teachings of Islam.

On the other hand, the Christian view of revelation and scriptures is significantly different from the Muslim witness. The Christians believe the Bible has been inspired (breathed in by God) but not dictated by God, that the imprint of human personality is part of the content of Biblical revelations, and that the Messiah (Jesus) himself is the *Injil* (Gospel).

However, according to Muslim witness, revelation which is contained in scriptures or Divine Books, is the true guidance that has been sent down (*tanzil*) directly from God. It is God's Word revealed to chosen prophets. Gifted personalities as the prophets were, their life and history did not form part of the Divine Message, or scriptural message. It is for the same reason that the *Hadith*, important as it is for Muslim belief, is not part of the Holy Qur'an.

It is only unfortunate that the Christians do not acknowledge the final, and perfect revelation of God—the Qur'an.

*'For no prophecy ever came by the impulse of man, but men moved by the Holy Spirit spoke from God'* (2 Peter 1:21).

# 18. The Prophets in History

## THE CHRISTIAN UNDERSTANDING

The Bible is a history book. It tells the story of God's redemptive acts in history. The Bible also contains the revealed interpretation of these redemptive acts. It is through the prophets and apostles that God interprets His redemptive acts in history.

We can illustrate Biblical revelation by using one example: the birth of the Messiah as recorded and interpreted by the Apostle Matthew (Matthew 1:18–2:23). Before Joseph and the virgin Mary were married, Mary was found to be with child through the Holy Spirit. An angel interpreted to Joseph and the virgin Mary the meaning of the virgin's miraculous conception. The promised Saviour was born in Bethlehem. Wise men from the east saw a special star and recognized that this was a sign from God that the Messiah (King) had been born. They came to Jerusalem in Judea with gifts seeking for the child. In Jerusalem they met with King Herod of Judea and scholars who knew the Old Testament prophecies concerning the Messiah. They were told that the Messiah was to be born in the nearby town of Bethlehem. They went on to Bethlehem where they found Jesus with Mary and Joseph. They praised God that the Saviour had been born, and gave Him costly gifts: gold, frankincense, and myrrh. An angel warned them not to return to Jerusalem, for King Herod wished to know where the baby was staying so that he could kill him. Later, when Herod heard that the wise men had returned to their homes through another way, he was furious and ordered the death of all the boy babies in Bethlehem who were two years old or younger. Nevertheless, Jesus was saved from death because an angel warned the family to flee into Egypt before Herod's troops arrived in Bethlehem. After Herod had died, Mary, Joseph, and the child Jesus returned to their homeland and lived in the town of Nazareth. All of this was a fulfillment of the Old Testament prophecies concerning the birth and childhood of Jesus the Messiah.

That is the story, briefly told. The story includes three revelation elements: event, response, interpretation. All three are inseparably merged together; all three are revelation. *The event* in the story is God's redemptive act: the birth of the Messiah. *The response* is two-fold: the wisemen believe, but King Herod does not believe; he fights against the child, against God's redemptive act, against God Himself. The *interpretation* of the story makes it meaningful: the Saviour has been born. Some people reject him. Others accept him. To believe or not to believe, that is the issue. This is the nature of all Biblical revelation: event—response—interpretation.

The Bible reveals that God invites us into a covenant relationship with Himself. He acts redemptively within our own historical experience. The Bible records countless descriptions of God's redemptive acts. Here are a few examples:

He saved Noah and his family from the flood.

He saved the life of the son of the Prophet Abraham through the sacrifice of a ram.

He appeared to the Prophet Moses in a burning bush.

He delivered the people of the covenant from slavery under Pharaoh.

He led them through the Red Sea on dry land.

He fed them manna in the wilderness when there was no food.

He gave them the Ten Commandments at Mount Sinai.

He gave them water from the rock in the desert.

He preserved their clothing and shoes.

The acts of God go on and on. He is involved redemptively in human experience. These acts of God, His redemptive involvement in history, is the central aspect of all Divine revelation. God is known by what He does; that is the focus of the Biblical view of revelation. Consequently, a major part of the Bible is a description of what God has done in history, as for example, the story of the birth of Jesus the Messiah.

The acts of God, however, never take place in a historical vacuum. Whenever God acts, people respond in acceptance or rejection, in belief or nonbelief, in repentance or rebellion. The Bible reveals that God's redemptive acts call for human response. Consequently, the Bible describes also the human response to God's redemptive acts. The Bible is a record of both God's encounter with man, and man's response to God. The descriptions of man's response to God reveal the nature of the human heart. We see ourselves in the story of the wicked king Herod who hated anyone who threatened his position. We also see ourselves in the wise men who sought for the truth. The Biblical description of the human response to God is an important aspect of revelation, because through it we come to recognize who we are and our own need for redemption.

The act of God—the human response: these two dimensions of God-man relationship are inseparable dimensions of Biblical revelation.

It is only through Divine revelation that we can really understand the meaning of the Divine-human encounter. This is the mission of the apostles and prophets of God. Through Divine inspiration God revealed to the apostles and prophets the meaning of the acts of God and man's response to those acts. We often read in the Bible that the prophet 'saw' or 'heard' the Word of the Lord (Isaiah 1:1, Obadiah 1:1, Micah 1:1, Habbakuk 1:1). This is Divine revelation. God revealed the true interpretation of His acts to the apostles and prophets. They proclaimed that interpretation through preaching, teaching, or writing. It is through the prophetic interpretation of God's saving acts in history that we recognize God's redemptive presence.

The Apostle Matthew recorded the event; he described the human response; he interpreted what was happening: His name is Jesus 'for He will save His people from their sins' (Matthew 1:21). That is Biblical revelation: history and interpretation. The act of God, the human response, the inspired interpretation, the three together are Biblical revelation.

## A MUSLIM RESPONSE

Muslims stress that the continued appearance of prophets at various times in history, among different peoples, shows the continuity of God's guidance, and His active interest in man's well-being in this world and the hereafter.

While Christians emphasize 'Divine inspiration' as the means by which God revealed the true interpretation of His acts, Muslims, while not ruling out Divine inspiration for prophets, are of the view that God sent down (*anzala, tanzil*) Divine revelation to His messengers. Allah gave the message to the angel Jibril, who communicated it in direct speech. The prophets expressed that direct speech exactly as they heard it from the angel. In the Qur'an, Allah uses the following terms for revelation: *anzala* (Qur'an 6:92), *uhiya* (Qur'an 6:94), *awha* (Qur'an 26:63), *nazzala* (Qur'an 25:1), *ata* (Qur'an 2:87), *tanzil* (Qur'an 36:5). All these terms suggest that He reveals the message or sends it down through an agent and not that He himself comes down (*nuzul*). All Divine revelation expresses the absolute legal sovereignty of Allah. The inspired knowledge of saints and mystics is far below and incomparable to the revelation of God's will through His prophets.

Prophetic revelation in Islam transcends history. That is to say, neither historical events, nor the human response to those events is in any sense revelation. Although the prophet stands in history, the revelation which he receives is not affected by his history. Revelation comes only from God. That is the Muslim witness.

## A CHRISTIAN CLARIFICATION

When Christians refer to the inspiration of Holy Scriptures, they mean that these writings have been 'breathed' by God through prophetic personhood. The concept is not equal to the more ordinary experience of inspired spirituality by mystics. The term *nuzul*, suggesting the coming down of Divine personal Presence, is a more appropriate interpretation of the Christian understanding of revelation, than is *tanzil*, sent down revelation. In a sense, all Biblical revelation has an incarnational quality about it. Revelation as *nuzul* involves a profound experience of God-man relationship, a relationship which neither compromises the sovereignty of God, nor the personhood of the man.

*. . . you shall call his name Jesus, for he will save his people from their sins'* (Matthew 1:21b).

# *19.* Jesus the Messiah

## THE CHRISTIAN WITNESS CONCERNING THE MESSIAH

The life and teaching of Jesus the Messiah is recorded in the four books of the Gospel: Matthew, Mark, Luke and John. These four books are biographical sketches of the Messiah, Who is the Gospel (*Injil*). Each of the four books of the Gospel were written by apostles or apostolic men. We believe that they are authentic witnesses.

In this chapter we shall give a brief biographical sketch of Jesus the Messiah, and then make some interpretive comments.

### The life and teaching of Jesus

As mentioned in the previous chapter, Jesus the Messiah was born in the town of Bethlehem in Judea in Palestine. The year was probably 4 B.C. Caesar Augustus was ruler of the Roman Empire. His birth by the virgin Mary had been foretold by the angel Gabriel who said,

The Holy Spirit will come upon you.
and the power of the Most High will overshadow you;
therefore the Child to be born will be called holy,
the Son of God (Luke 1:35).

Just before Jesus' birth, Mary and Joseph had travelled about 200 kilometers south from Nazareth in Galilee to Bethlehem in Judea for a Roman census. Because all lodging places were filled, they had to stay in a cattle stable. That is where Jesus was born. Angels announced His birth to shepherds on the nearby hills. These herdsmen came to see Jesus, and found Him with Mary and Joseph, just as the angels had said. Later wise men from the east also came to see Jesus. In the last chapter we described their visit, and the subsequent flight of Joseph, Mary and Jesus into Egypt to escape Herod's anger.

After returning from Egypt, the family settled in Nazareth in Galilee. That is where Jesus grew up, probably as a carpenter, for that was the occupation of Joseph. We do not know much about His boyhood. Only one incident is recorded in the Gospel; He went with Joseph and Mary to Jerusalem when He was twelve to worship the Lord. During that visit He astonished the religious leaders with His understanding of the Scriptures.

Jesus the Messiah began His public ministry when He was about thirty years of age. The event which marked the beginning of His ministry was His baptism in the river Jordan by John the Baptist (John the Baptist is known as the Prophet Yahiya by Muslims). The Gospel as recorded by Luke describes Jesus' baptism in this way:

> . . . when Jesus also had been baptized and was praying, the heaven was opened, and the Holy Spirit descended upon Him in bodily form, as a dove, and a voice came from heaven, 'Thou art My beloved Son; with Thee I am well pleased' (Luke 3:21,22).

Immediately after His baptism, Jesus was led by the Spirit of God into the wilderness where He fasted for forty days. After that Satan tempted Him severely: He tempted Jesus to turn stones to bread. He tempted him to prove His power by jumping off a pinnacle of the temple. Jesus was tempted to bow down before Satan, and as a reward he would be given all the kingdoms of the world. These temptations are signs of the common human temptations to lust for wealth, power and fame. Jesus quoted the Old Testament showing that these temptations were against the revealed Word of God. Finally Satan left Him, and the angels of God came to minister to Him.

After the period of temptation, Jesus began His public ministry, which lasted about three years. He travelled considerably in Judea and Galilee, but also crossed the national boundaries into regions such as Decapolis north of Galilee.

It is impossible to capture the breadth and meaning of Jesus the Messiah in a few paragraphs. He opened His ministry in His home town of Nazareth by startling the normal Sabbath congregational worship in the local synagogue with a reading from the Prophet Isaiah:

> The Spirit of the Lord is upon Me,
>> because He has annointed Me to proclaim good news to the poor.
> He has sent Me to proclaim release to the captives
>> and recovering of sight to the blind,

to set at liberty those who are oppressed,
to proclaim the acceptable year of the Lord (Luke 4:18,19).

After reading, He proclaimed, 'Today this scripture has been fulfilled in your hearing' (Luke 4:21). In this manner Jesus announced that in Him the Kingdom of God had broken into human history. The new covenant was established. Jesus the Messiah demonstrated the breakthrough of God's Kingdom throughout the rest of His ministry.

### Jesus was a miracle worker

He healed the blind, lepers, lame, and deaf. He cast out multitudes of evil spirits. He raised the dead. On one occasion He fed five thousand men, besides women and children, with only five loaves of bread and two small fishes. Another time He fed four thousand men, besides women and children, with seven loaves of bread and several small fishes. In His hands, the food was multiplied. Once He also walked from land across the water to meet and comfort His disciples who were caught in a storm in the middle of the Sea of Galilee. He calmed the storm. The people gave joyous witness that He was 'mighty in deed' (Luke 24:19).

### Jesus as an outstanding teacher

He used parables with great effectiveness. The parable is a story from ordinary life which communicates truth. Many of His parables communicated the meaning of the Kingdom of God. Some are short: 'The Kingdom of heaven is like leaven which a woman took and hid in three measures of meal, till it was all leavened' (Matthew 13:33). Others are more lengthy: The prodigal son who left his father's house, squandered his wealth and health in riotous living, and when he came to his senses returned to his father, who saw him when he was still a great way off, and ran to meet him. The father embraced his son and ordered a great feast. The older son who had never left home was furious that his lost younger brother had been welcomed home with joy and feasting.

Jesus also taught through dialogue. He asked questions of people, and led them into the truth as they sought the answers to the questions He asked. Jesus was a great preacher too. Audiences of several thousands would sit for many hours listening to His sermons, and '. . .the crowds were astonished at His teaching, for

He taught them as one who had authority, and not as their scribes' (Matthew 7:28,29).

## Opposition to Jesus

Slowly opposition developed against Jesus. This happened for several reasons:

*First,* Jesus was ruthlessly critical of all forms of false religion. He condemned religious hypocrisy, and he welcomed sinners to be his friends. He declared, 'I have not come to call the righteous but sinners to repentance' (Luke 5:32). This angered the religious leaders who had proud and superior attitudes.

*Second,* Jesus forgave sins. The religious leaders were furious, because they said that only God can forgive sins. Nevertheless, Jesus affirmed that '. . .the Son of man has authority on earth to forgive sins' (Matthew 9:6).

*Third,* Jesus said, 'I and the Father are one' (John 10:30). When Jesus said that, the religious leaders tried to stone Him, because they accused him of blasphemy; but Jesus pointed out that no one could do the works that He did unless God was in him. He said that the works which He did proved that '. . .the Father is in me, and I am in the Father' (John 10:38).

*Fourth,* Jesus proclaimed that the Kingdom of God had come. Remember that at this time Palestine was under the colonial rule of Rome. The Jewish leaders thought that the meaning of the Kingdom of God was political independence from Rome. Many of the Galilean Jews tried to force Jesus to become king. They were disappointed, because He refused to become the kind of king they desired. He did not lead a military insurrection against Roman colonial rule, and consequently, in disappointment and frustration, many turned against Him.

## The crucifixion and resurrection

All of these cross currents of opposition increased during the last months of Jesus' ministry. Finally He headed south from Galilee where, as mentioned above, a popular movement had attempted to install Him as the ruler of the Jews. As He travelled slowly south to Jerusalem in Judea, He warned His disciples that He would be crucified. This prophesy was fulfilled. At the Passover festival in Jerusalem, He was arrested and tried in both the Jewish and Roman courts. Although no two witnesses could agree on the charges, He was finally condemned to death. Mark records the trial in the Jewish court in this way:

Again the high priest asked Him, 'Are You the Christ, the Son of the Blessed?'

And Jesus said, 'I am; and you will see the Son of man sitting at the right hand of Power, and coming with the clouds of heaven.'

And the high priest tore his mantle, and said, 'Why do we still need witnesses: You have heard His blasphemy. What is your decision?'

And they all condemned Him as deserving death (Mark 14:61–64).

Although the Roman authorities in the Roman court saw no reason why He should be crucified, under mob pressure, the government finally accepted a charge that He claimed to be the King of the Jews. That was the charge which was nailed to the cross above His head when He was crucified.

Each of the Gospel writers described the crucifixion. Jesus was beaten. He was mocked and slapped. They put a crown of thorn on His head, and beat it into His skull. Finally He was nailed to the cross between two criminals. For three midday hours, darkness covered the land. 'At last He said, 'It is finished!', and He bowed His head and gave up His spirit' (John 19:30).

Friends of Jesus buried Him in a new tomb carved in rock which was near the place of the crucifixion. The tomb was owned by a rich man, Joseph of Arimathea. He was in the grave until dawn on the third day. Then He arose from the dead. Several women, and then some of His disciples, discovered on Sunday morning that the grave was empty. After that Jesus appeared several times to His disciples. First He appeared to one of the women, Mary Magdalene. Then to two of the disciples walking on the road to Emmaus. Then to more of the disciples. He appeared at least eleven times during the next forty days. He ate with the disciples and conversed with them. They knew that He was the risen Messiah. Finally He took them to a hill outside Jerusalem, and was received into heaven.

In a later chapter, we will discuss the continuing presence of the glorified Messiah in the life and ministry of the Church. In this chapter we have limited our discussion to a brief review of some of the highlights of the earthly ministry of Jesus, and the crucifixion and resurrection events. The life, death and resurrection of Jesus the Messiah is an astonishing and marvellous event. Many details of His life had been carefully and accurately foretold by the Old

Testament prophets. Nevertheless, for many people He seems unbelievable. The Apostle John, however, writes, '...these are written that you may believe that Jesus is the Christ, the Son of God, and that believing you may have life in His name' (John 20:31). Later the Apostle says that he is '...the disciple who is bearing witness to these things, and who has written these things; and ...knows that his testimony is true' (John 21:24).

## Who is Jesus the Messiah?

It is impossible to interpret Jesus the Messiah in a few short pages. Thousands of books have been written, hundreds of new books are published every year which attempt to interpret Him. All are inadequate. Certainly these few pages are also insufficient. Yet Christians must attempt to give witness, although we confess that the witness which we give cannot adequately convey the mystery and the depth of who Jesus is.

We shall attempt to interpret Jesus briefly by introducing some of the names which the Biblical writers have used to describe Him. These names give different portraits of Jesus. Each is significant and true. Each is also inadequate. Yet the names can be helpful signs pointing us toward a recognition of who Jesus is.

### The Son of Man

Jesus almost always referred to Himself as the Son of Man. This shows that He is an authentic human being. He is the true Son of Adam. He identifies with us totally. He was born into a poor home. He became a refugee when less than two years of age. He worked for a living as a carpenter. He experienced suffering and mis-understanding. He is a real man who understands us fully. He is Son of Man.

### The Suffering Servant

Several hundred years before the Messiah came, God had re-vealed to the Prophet Isaiah that the coming Messiah would be a suffering servant. The Prophet wrote:

> He was despised and rejected by men; a man of sorrows, and acquainted with grief; and as one from whom men hide their faces He was despised, and we esteemed Him not (Isaiah 53:3).

In the Messiah we see this prophecy fulfilled. He served mankind as a humble servant.

On one occasion the Messiah revealed a deep sign of His servant ministry, by washing His disciples feet! In Palestine it was normal for the servant of the household to wash the feet of the master of the home when he entered the house after a day's work, or returned home after a journey. But Jesus took the place of the servant. He took a towel and washed and dried the feet of his beloved disciples! They were astonished, but he told them, 'I have given you an example, that you should do as I have done to you' (John 13:15).

All who recognize Jesus as the Messiah, should also become servants to one another, just as Jesus became a servant to His disciples and the people of His day. In fact, Jesus gave Himself in servant ministry so completely that He suffered in doing good. He walked the paths of Palestine ministering to the needs of hundreds and thousands of people. His suffering servanthood is climaxed by the crucifixion wherein He poured out His life for our sakes. Jesus the Messiah is the perfect Servant Who gave His life in service for mankind. Through His suffering redemptive servant-hood, we are healed and made whole. As Servant, He provides us with all we need.

### The Lamb

When the Messiah came to John the Baptist to be baptized, John cried out, 'Behold the Lamb of God Who takes away the sin of the world' (John 1:29)! In most human societies, people offer animal sacrifices, hoping for the forgiveness of their sins. These sacrifices are signs which help us to understand that mankind needs to be redeemed through a perfect sacrifice. Christians believe that these offerings are a sign pointing to the Messiah Who gave His life for our redemption from sin. He is the perfect Lamb of God. Through his sacrificial death and resurrection, we are for-given and redeemed (Revelation 5:9).

### The Son of God

This name was not invented by the disciples. Twice in Jesus' ministry He is addressed as 'My Son' by a voice from heaven. First at His baptism a voice came from heaven saying, 'Thou art My beloved Son; with Thee I am well pleased' (Luke 3:22). Again at the climax of Jesus' ministry, He and three of His disciples were in the Mount of Transfiguration alone. A cloud of glory covered them, the prophets Moses and Elijah miraculously appeared, and then a voice came from the cloud saying, 'This is my Son, my Chosen; listen to Him' (Luke 9:35)! These two events reveal that God Himself addressed Jesus as 'My Son'.

Jesus accepted the name Son of God for Himself. On one occasion, He asked His disciples who they believed He was. We read:

> Simon Peter replied, 'You are the Christ, the Son of the living God.' And Jesus answered him, 'Blessed are you, Simon Bar-Jona! For flesh and blood has not revealed this to you, but My Father Who is in heaven' (John 16:151–7).

The name, Son of God, reveals a perfect fellowship of love between Jesus and God the Father. We have already mentioned that man is created in the image of God, that Adam and Eve were created as sons and daughters of God. Before they disobeyed, they knew and enjoyed complete spiritual fellowship with God. Throughout the Old Testament, people were invited into a covenant relationship with God. God was pleased to invite people to become his covenant children. The people of the covenant were invited to accept God as their heavenly Father. Jesus, as the Son of God, is the One Who experienced a perfect God-man relationship.

Jesus' experience of fellowship with God was perfect. He is the perfect image of God. He is the perfect human being. He is the One whose relationship with God is so clear and perfect and open and right that He is indeed the Son of God. So intimate is His relationship with the Father, that Jesus could say with absolute humility and truthfulness, 'I and the Father are one' (John 10:30).

### Immanuel

The Prophet Isaiah, writing many centuries before the birth of the Messiah, prophesied that His name shall be called 'Immanuel' (Isaiah 7:14). The Apostle Matthew recalls this prophesy, when he tells of the virgin birth of Jesus. Matthew points out that Isaiah's prophesy affirms that the One born of the virgin shall be Immanuel, which in the Hebrew language means 'God with us' (Matthew 1:23).

The witness of the New Testament is that God has revealed Himself fully in Jesus Christ. He is 'God with us'. The Apostolic witness throughout the New Testament is that 'God was in Christ'. The Apostle Paul writes under the inspiration of God, 'He [Christ] is the image of the invisible God, the first-born of all creation; . . . For in Him all the fullness of God was pleased to dwell, . . .' (Colossians 1:15,19). Jesus Himself said, 'He who has seen Me has seen the Father; how can you say, 'Show us the Father'?' (John 14:9). God has made Himself known to us in Jesus Christ. Because of Jesus, God is not a stranger.

## The Word

Jesus is also called the Word of God. The Gospel witness, according to the Apostle John, begins,

> In the beginning was the Word, and the Word was with God, and the Word was God. He was in the beginning with God; all things were made through Him, and without Him was not anything made that was made. . . . And the Word became flesh and dwelt among us, full of grace and truth; we have beheld His glory, glory as of the only Son from the Father (John 1:1–3,14).

We know that God never sleeps. He is always expressing Himself, and God's self expression is creative. The self expression of God is the Word, and when God speaks, creation happens. Through God's Speech or Word, the universe is created. In Jesus the Messiah, God's eternal self expression, His everlasting Word, has become flesh.

The Word of God is eternal, just as God is eternal. It is for this reason that the Messiah, as the incarnation of the eternal Word of God, could say, '. . . before Abraham was, I am' (John 8:58).

The Messiah, as the incarnation of the Word of God, is eternal and uncreated. He is not begotten by God, because He is the eternal uncreated word of God. 'Who . . . was in the beginning with God; . . . (John 1:2a).

Jesus the Messiah is the living eternal Word of God in human form. The Bible is God's written Word, but Jesus the Messiah is the incarnation of the eternal personal Living Word of God. The Apostle John wrote:

> That which was from the beginning, which we have heard, which we have seen with our eyes, which we have looked upon and touched with our hands, concerning the Word of Life— . . . that which we have seen and heard we proclaim also to you . . . (1 John 1:1,3).

The purpose of the Bible is to reveal to us the Living Word, Who is Jesus the Messiah.

Jesus said, 'You search the scriptures, because you think that in them you have eternal life; and it is they that bear witness to me; . . . ' (John 5:39).

Many other names are also given to Jesus: Rabbi or Teacher, Prophet, King, Lord, Saviour, Judge, Redeemer. We could add to the list some of the 'I am' statements of Jesus: I am the resurrection; I am the life; I am the truth; I am the way. We readily recognize that Jesus Christ cannot be fully captured by any name or cluster of titles. The Christian witness is that we are invited to meet Jesus the Messiah and respond to Him with joy.

## A MUSLIM RESPONSE

Muslims have great respect and love for Jesus (Isa) the Messiah. He is one of the greatest prophets of Allah. To deny the prophethood of Jesus is to deny Islam. Muslims sincerely believe that Jesus (PBUH) was born of a virgin mother, Maryam (Mary), by Allah's Divine decree. He is referred to in the Qur'an as the son of Mary.

The Qur'an teaches that the coming of the Messiah was 'glad tidings' (Qur'an 3:45). It describes his birth in this manner:

> Then we sent unto her [Mary], Our spirit and it assumed for her the likeness of Man. She said Lo! . . . He said I am only a messenger of thy Lord, that I may bestow on thee a faultless boy. She said: How can I have a boy when no mortal hath touched me . . . He said: (So it will be) Thy Lord saith. It is easy for me. And (it will be) that we may make of him a revelation for mankind and a mercy from us, and it is a thing ordained (Qur'an 19:7–21).

On the other hand, Muslims are genuinely opposed to the belief by Christians that Isa (PBUH) was Divine or 'Son of God'. The basis of Muslim objection is Qur'anic. Allah says: 'It is not befitting to (the Majesty of Allah) that He should beget a son. Glory be to him, when he determines a matter, He only says to it 'Be' and it is there' (Qur'an 5:75).*

---

*See also Qur'an 19:88–93, 18:4–5, 2:116–117, 6:101–102.

The Qur'an testifies that Isa (PBUH) commanded the children of Israel, to whom he was a messenger, to worship 'Allah, mine Lord and your Lord'. So to the Muslims, Isa (PBUH) was human like the earlier prophets, and was not an incarnation of God. The Qur'an explicitly states: 'No son did Allah beget nor is there any god along with Him.'

This is the point where Muslims and Christians painfully part company. The issue is deeply theological and anthropological. The Christian view of incarnation seems to compromise God's transcendence and sovereignty while at the same time exalting a mere man to God-like status. By denying the incarnation, Islam is really affirming both the absolute transcendence of God *and* the rightful status of man as the servant and *khalifa* of God on earth.

The gulf between Christians and Muslims is further widened by the Christian silence on and non-recognition of Muhammad (PBUH) as the Seal of Prophets, and the final guidance (the Qur'an) that was revealed to him by God. Yet recently Deedat has convincingly shown that the Bible says something about Muhammad (PBUH)—in Deuteronomy chapter 18, verse 18, which reads: 'I will raise them a prophet from among their brethren, like unto thee, and I will put my words in his mouth, and he shall speak unto them all that I shall command him.'*

*Ahmad Deedat, *What the Bible Says About Muhammad*, Durban, Islamic Propagations Centre, 49 Madressa Arcade, N.D., pp. 1–28. In this book the author shows that in all ways Muhammad (PBUH) was like Moses and Jesus was unlike Moses. Moses and his people, the Jews, are here addressed as a racial entity and as such their brethren would undoubtedly be the Arabs, all stemming from the same father, Abraham, but with different mothers, Hagar and Sarah. He also points out that Muhammad (PBUH) (unlike Jesus) was illiterate and the words (revelation) were actually put into his mouth as exactly foretold in the prophecy '... and I will put my words in his mouth ...' (Deut. 18:18). Muhammad (PBUH) is brother to the Israelites because he was a descendant of Ismailil the son of Abraham.

## A CHRISTIAN CLARIFICATION

Christians agree with Muslims that God did not 'beget' a son. To conceive of God as begetting a son would be a gross evil for it would suggest polytheism, and, furthermore, be a base anthropomorphism. Christians agree that God did not beget nor ever shall beget a son.

Jesus the Messiah, as Son of God, reveals something completely different. It reveals a perfect relationship between God and the Messiah, the Sonship of Christ is a description of perfect love and fellowship between God and the Messiah.

Recall that Christians believe that the Messiah is the incarnation of the eternal Word of God. God does not beget his Word! His Word is eternal, co-existent with God, the perfect self expression of God.

The two concepts of Word and Sonship need to be kept together in order to understand the Christian witness that the Messiah is Immanuel, God with us.

*'And all flesh shall see the salvation of God'* (Luke 3:6).


# 20. Salvation

## THE CHRISTIAN EXPERIENCE

Nicodemus was a respected leader of the Jews who came to Jesus
secretly at night to learn about salvation.

Jesus told him, 'Truly, truly, I say to you, unless one is born
anew, he cannot see the Kingdom of God.'

Nicodemus replied, 'How can a man be born when he is old:
Can he enter a second time into his mother's womb and be born?'

Jesus said, 'Truly, truly, I say to you, unless one is born of water
and the Spirit, he cannot enter the kingdom of God. That which
is born of the flesh is flesh, and that which is born of the Spirit is
spirit.'

Nicodemus asked, 'How can this be?'

And Jesus continued, 'God so loved the world that He gave
His only Son, that whoever believes in Him should not perish,
but have eternal life. For God sent the Son into the world, not to
condemn the world, but that the world might be saved through
Him.' (Read the whole conversation in John 3:1–21.)

This conversation reveals to us that God, our heavenly Father,
sent His Son into the world to save mankind. Those who receive
His Son, the Messiah, experience a new birth. This salvation
experience is a miracle of the Spirit of God. God as Father, Son,
and Spirit are united in loving redemptive action. Our acceptance
and experience of the Trinity love of God is salvation.

Is that hard to understand? Don't worry. Nicodemus was
perplexed too. Let us look more carefully at the redemptive work
of God as Father, Son, and Holy Spirit. We need to believe and
receive God's saving redemptive action as Father, Son, and Holy
Spirit in order to experience salvation.

*God our heavenly Father* created us in the image of God. This
means that we are most truly human when we live in joyous
fellowship with God. But Adam and Eve and all of us have turned
away from our heavenly Father. Yet God has never left us.
Throughout history He has repeatedly invited people to become

His covenant children of faith, to repent and enter into the experience of redemption and salvation.

Nevertheless, our sinfulness always prevents us from experiencing perfect fellowship with God. We are unable to live righteously because we are sinful.

The Prophet Isaiah lamented: 'We have all become like one who is unclean, and all our righteous deeds are like a polluted garment' (Isaiah 64:6). Our sinfulness separates us from God. Event he Prophet Moses could not meet God face to face (Exodus 33:18–23). We are ashamed and fearful. We know that we are guilty. We experience insincerity and hypocrisy. Mankind has frequently tried to cover his guilt by animal sacrifices or offerings. Yet the sense of a broken and imperfect relationship with God is always present.

We know that our sin has separated us from God. Although God invites people into covenant, mankind fails to live within the covenant. Although God commands repentance, we seldom hear or obey His call.

Consequently, in order to save and redeem us from sin, God entered history in *Jesus Christ*, His beloved Son. Three dimensions of Jesus's life and work must be considered if we are to understand salvation:

*First*, the life of Jesus the Messiah reveals the Kingdom of God. In fact, He is the breakthrough of the Kingdom of God into history. He is the new creation, the new Adam, the Adam from heaven, Who is the kind of Adam we should be (1 Corinthians 15:45–50). God commanded Adam to have dominion over the earth, but Adam and all mankind have failed to have perfect dominion over earth. Yet it is not so with Jesus. The Messiah, the new Adam from heaven, has absolute dominion over nature. He walks on water. He calms the raging storm. He heals the sick. He multiplies food. Jesus does have dominion over the earth.

We also know that we should live sinless lives, but we don't live righteously. We should establish justice, but instead we often neglect the right of those who are weaker than we are. Yet Jesus was righteous. He lived justice. He never sinned. Jesus is the kind of Adam we should be. He is Lord of nature. He is the sinless One, He is the just One. He is the Kingdom of God within human history. He is the recreation, the authentic breakthrough of the gracious will of God for all mankind. Jesus relates to everyone with perfect power, authority, justice, and love. He is the authentic man. In him the Kingdom of God is fulfilled. In him we perceive salvation (Hebrews 2:6–9).

*Second*, the crucifixion and death of Jesus the Messiah reveals the love of God and the inner mystery of the Kingdom of God. Because God is love, He will never forcefully impose His will on mankind. Rather than force us to obey Him, God has chosen to accept all our hostility and violence and hate upon Himself. God in the Messiah accepts our rebellion, with suffering self-giving love.

The whole of mankind is represented at the crucifixion of Jesus the Messiah: the religious leaders and the politicians; the mob and the common man; the educated, wealthy, and professional; the poor and dispossessed; women and men; slaves and free; Europe, Asia, Africa, the world. All are involved in the tragic crucifixion of Jesus. As He hangs on the cross, they wag their heads and mock, but Jesus holds no bitterness or revenge. Instead He cries out, 'Father forgive them' (Luke 23:34). In that cry of forgiveness, we recognize the horror of our sin and also the love and forgiveness of God. Why rebel against God if He forgives, even when we are crucifying the Messiah, the Anointed One, the altogether righteous One, the Son of God? The cross reveals the love and forgiveness of God in the most profound possible way. In that forgiveness, we find that we are accepted by God.

At the moment when Jesus yielded His life on the cross, the curtain in the temple in Jerusalem was miraculously torn in two from the top to the bottom (Luke 23:44–45). This curtain was the barrier within the temple which separated the Holy Place from the Holy of Holies. It was believed that the glory of God was present in the Holy of Holies. Only the high priest was permitted into the presence of the glory of God, and that only once a year. But when Jesus was crucified, that curtain hiding the glory of God from human view was torn in two. That tear in the curtain is a sign that all the barriers between God and man have been removed through the death of Jesus Christ. We are forgiven. We are accepted. We can now address God with joy and confidence as 'Father'. The barrier which our sinfulness had created between God and us is removed forever.

By giving His life on the cross, Jesus the Messiah gave Himself as the perfect sacrifice for our sins (Hebrews 8, 9, 10). We have mentioned that many peoples offer sacrifices of offerings in the hope that these will help to cover their sins and save them from evil. In the Old Testament, the people were commanded to offer a multitude of sacrifices. Even Abraham offered a ram in sacrifice, and in this way the life of his son was saved by God. These were a sign pointing to the perfect sacrifice for sin Who is Jesus the Messiah. We know that we deserve punishment, because we are sinful. Jesus bore the punishment for our sin. In Christ, God has accepted onto Himself the grief and shame and punishment of our sinfulness. We know that 'the wages of sin is death' (Romans 6:23). Jesus has suffered death for us so that we can experience life. We read,

But He was wounded for our transgressions,
  He was bruised for our iniquities;
Upon Him was the chastisement that made us whole,
and with His stripes we are healed (Isaiah 53:5).

In the *third* place, we experience salvation through the resurrection of Jesus the Messiah. When we separate ourselves from God, we experience death. Satan is the prince of the powers of death. He and all the evil angels and spirits whom he leads are champions of death. Satan was pleased when Jesus was crucified. Death is his business. Nevertheless, God raised Jesus Christ from the dead. The resurrection of the Messiah is the defeat of death. The power of Satan has been broken. Death shall not win. Resurrection and life shall triumph.

God wants us to experience the new life revealed in the resurrection of Jesus Christ. Just as the Messiah rose from the dead, so we who believe shall also rise from death into life everlasting. Although our biological bodies may die, at the end of history we shall all be raised with new and glorified bodies, just as Jesus was raised from the dead (1 Corinthians 15).

Just as the resurrection of Jesus Christ represents the defeat of Satan and the evil spirits who are the champions of death, so we also experience victory over all the evil spiritual powers of death, when we open our lives to the power of the risen Messiah. God has put all powers under the authority of the risen glorified Messiah. We who believe in Him experience release from fear and freedom from slavery to all evil spirits and powers (Ephesians 1:15-23).

God has appointed the risen Messiah to be the intercessor between God and man. The Bible says, 'So also Christ did not exalt Himself to be made a high priest, but was appointed by (God)' (Hebrews 5:5). God has appointed the glorified, risen Messiah to be our intercessor, because He has lived among us and understands us perfectly. He experienced the same temptations and sorrows we do, yet He never sinned (Hebrews 2:18). Because

God has appointed the Messiah to be the perfect mediator between God and man, Christians pray to their heavenly Father in the name of Jesus the Messiah. Jesus Himself has promised, 'My Father will give you whatever you ask in My name' (John 16:23a, NIV).

*The Spirit of God* is also involved in our experience of salvation. Jesus told Nicodemus that he must be born of the water and the Spirit. What is the work of the Spirit in bringing salvation?

Remember that it was the Spirit who revealed the Word of the Lord to the ancient prophets of the Old Testament. It is this same Spirit Who reveals the truth of God to us today. All that we have said, concerning God and the life and work of Jesus the Messiah, is meaningless unless we are open to the voice and witness of the Spirit of God. It is through the Holy Spirit that we are guided into all truth. It is through the Spirit that the life of the risen, triumphant Messiah becomes part of our own experience. When we repent and believe, it is the Spirit Who recreates the true image of God in us.

God had promised, through the Prophet Jeremiah, that He would make a new covenant with mankind, by creating a new heart in man. This is a new creation. It is the Spirit of God who performs this miracle of grace and power in the believer. In the New Testament we read, 'This is the covenant that I will make with them after those days says the Lord; I will put my laws on their hearts, and write them on their minds, I will remember their sins and their misdeeds no more' (Hebrews 10:16,17).

Jesus the Messiah called this new covenant and new creation, the new birth. When we accept God's saving love as revealed in Jesus the Messiah, the Spirit of God begins to recreate us. We begin to live within the Kingdom of God. We begin to experience the new creation from heaven which Jesus represented so perfectly. We become more and more like Jesus. We become people who are free to love with joy.

We experience salvation when we receive God's love and forgiveness which is revealed in Jesus the Messiah, and which is present with us now through the Holy Spirit of God. It is in the life, death, and resurrection of Jesus Christ that God's love is perfectly revealed. It is through the Holy Spirit that we experience His love personally. God sent His Son into the world so 'that the world might be saved through Him' (John 3:17). And God has sent the Holy Spirit, '. . .the Spirit of His Son into our hearts, crying "Abba! Father" ' (Galatians 4:7). The one true God Whom we experience as Father, Son, and Holy Spirit, in perfect unity, perfect love, perfect oneness, redeems us and saves us through his self-giving love.

In the Hebrew language, the name Jesus means Yahweh Saves. The salvation which we experience through believing in Jesus Christ includes:

Right and joyous fellowship with God; reconciliation with God.
Reconciliation with our fellowmen.
Forgiveness of sins.
A new creation or new birth of the true image of God within us.
Personal wholeness and blessing.
The experience of the love of God and the joyous privilege of addressing God as 'Father'.
The defeat of death, eternal life, and the assurance of bodily resurrection from the dead.
Victory over sin and all the evil spirits and powers.
Participation in the Kingdom of God, now and eternally.

We could say much more. In its simplest and most profound meaning, salvation is the experience of the love of God. We experience salvation by believing in and committing ourselves totally to Jesus the Messiah, Who is the One through Whom God has revealed Himself as the Saviour Who loves us redemptively.

After Christ had risen from the dead and had been received into heaven, two Christian leaders, Paul and Silas by name, were put in jail for casting evil spirits out of a slave girl in Philippi in Macedonia, Greece. That night an earthquake struck, and the doors of the jail flew open. The jailer was about to kill himself, for he feared that the prisoners had fled, but Paul and Silas called and refrained him. None of the prisoners had fled.

Then the jailer asked, 'What must I do to be saved?'

Paul and Silas answered, 'Believe on the Lord Jesus and you will be saved, you and your household' (Acts 16:30,31).

The Christian witness is that people, who believe in Jesus the Messiah, experience salvation and they become part of the new covenant community which is called the Church. In the next chapter we shall discuss the nature and work of the Church. We shall also comment on God's plan for the Church and the role of the Church within the Kingdom of God.

## A MUSLIM RESPONSE

From the Christian experience, salvation is basically centred on the mission and crucifixion of Jesus Christ. This view is indeed in contrast to the Muslim experience.

According to Islam, Jesus Christ (Isa) (PBUH), son of Mary, was a great Apostle of God. He was made to follow the footsteps of the prophets and to confirm the Law which was sent down before him. He was given the Gospel (*Injil*), as the light and guidance for mankind. The Qur'an relates: 'And we will make him a Messenger unto the children of Israel, saying: Lo I come unto you with a sign from your Lord. And I come confirming that which was before me of the Torah' (Qur'an 3:49–50).

The Prophet Isa (PBUH), like many prophets before him, performed miracles, e.g. curing the insane and the blind, curing the lepers and raising the dead. He did these miracles by Allah's will. They were meant to serve as proof of the truth of his mission. The important role bestowed on the Prophet Isa (PBUH) did not make him 'Son of God' or single him out as the *only* saviour for mankind. In fact the Prophet Isa (PBUH) was only a servant and messenger of Allah. The Qur'an says: 'Not one of the beings in the heavens and earth but must come to (Allah) most gracious as servant' (Qur'an 19:93).

The Christian witness that man is forgiven because of the crucifixion of Jesus is not in line with the Muslim belief. The end of the Prophet Isa (PBUH) on earth is blanketed in mystery, and many Muslims prefer not to go beyond the explanation given in the Qur'an. On this issue the Qur'an tells us:

> That they said (in boast); We killed Christ Jesus, the son of Mary, the Messenger of God! But they killed him not, nor crucified him, but it was made to appear to them; and those who differ, therein are full of doubts, with no (certain) knowledge, but only conjecture to follow. For surety, they killed him not. Nay, Allah raised him unto Himself; and Allah is ever Mighty wise (Qur'an 4:157-158).

According to the true belief of Islam, it would seem most inappropriate for the Messiah to die through a shameful crucifixion. God, who is just, would not permit the righteous Messiah to suffer in that manner. Muslims believe that Allah saved the Messiah from the ignomy of crucifixion much as Allah also saved the Seal of the Prophets from ignomy following the Hijra.

Furthermore, Islam does not identify with the Christian conviction that man needs to be redeemed. The Christian belief in the redemptive sacrificial death of Christ does not fit the Islamic view that man has always been fundamentally good, and that God loves and forgives those who obey His will.

Islam is the way of peace. The Muslim view, which is in total contrast to the Christian experience, is that man experiences peace through total submission to God's guidance and mercy. Jesus Christ (PBUH), like many prophets before him, and Muhammad (PBUH) the Seal of Prophets, have all been examples of God's mercy to humanity.

## A CHRISTIAN CLARIFICATION

It may be that the Christian and the Muslim view of the crucifixion of Christ is more close together than appears on the surface. The Gospel emphasizes that Jesus the Messiah gave His life. He said,

. . .I lay down My life, that I may take it again. No one takes it from Me, but I lay it down of My Own accord. I have power to lay it down, and I have power to take it again; this charge I have received from My Father' (John 10:17,18).

The crucifixion of Christ is a drama of supreme self giving. The Messiah Himself gives His life; no one can take it from Him, for certainly no one can slay the eternal Word of God. And although He gave Himself unto death on the cross at the hands of evil men, they, nevertheless, could not destroy Him, for He arose from the grave. Certainly Christians would agree that death cannot be triumphant over the Messiah. In His resurrection, He has triumphed over death.

*'. . . the household of God, which is the church of the living God, the pillar and bulwark of the truth'* (1 Timothy 3:15b).

# 21. The Church

### THE CHRISTIAN COMMUNITY

The Church was created by God at the feast of Pentecost fifty days after the death and resurrection of Jesus the Messiah. During His last resurrection appearance, Jesus told His disciples to wait in Jerusalem until they had received the Holy Spirit (Acts 1:4,5). Forty days after His resurrection, Jesus the Messiah was received into heaven, and the disciples obeyed Jesus and remained in an upper room in Jerusalem, waiting for the Holy Spirit. They spent the time praying, fasting, and waiting. About 120 people were present (Acts 1).

The disciples waited for ten days until the Pentecost festival. This feast was a Jewish celebration of thanksgiving for the first fruit of the harvest. It was on Pentecost day that God blessed the disciples with the Holy Spirit. We read:

> And suddenly a sound came from heaven like the rush of a mighty wind, and it filled all the house where they were sitting. And there appeared to them tongues as of fire, distributed and resting on each one of them. And they were all filled with the Holy Spirit and began to speak in other tongues, as the Spirit gave them utterance (Acts 2:2–4).

The sound of the event was heard outside, and people from different parts of Jerusalem came to hear and see what was happening. Each person heard the Gospel proclaimed in his own native tongue: 'Parthians and Medes and Elamites and residents of Mesopotamia, Judea and Cappadocia, Pontus and Asia, Phyrgia and Pamphylia, Egypt and the parts of Libya belonging to Cyrene, and visitors from Rome, both Jews and proselytes, Cretans and Arabians, . . .' (Acts 2:9–11). They were amazed, because miraculously, as the disciples praised the Lord, each person heard the Gospel (*Injil*) in his mother tongue.

The **Apostle Peter** stood and began to preach the Gospel to the assembled. After the people had heard the Gospel, they cried out, 'Brethren, what shall we do?"

Peter answered, 'Repent, and be baptized every one of you in the name of Jesus Christ for the forgiveness of your sins; and you shall receive the gift of the Holy Spirit' (Acts 2:37,38).

The people responded to the Gospel, and about 3000 were baptized that day. This is the beginning of the Christian Church, which has now grown to include hundreds of millions of people living in almost every country on earth. What is this new community of faith which was created by God at Pentecost nearly 2000 years ago? What is the nature of the Church which attracts millions of new believers into its fellowship every year? Who is the Church?

## Believing people are the Church

We have already mentioned that during His ministry, Jesus called twelve disciples to follow him. These men came from different backgrounds, several were fishermen by trade, another was a tax collector, at least one had been a guerilla freedom fighter (Luke 6:13,14). He formed the disciples into a new community who recognized that Jesus Christ is Lord.

The faith of the disciples is revealed in the response of Peter to Jesus' question, 'Who do you say that I am?'

Peter answered, 'You are the Christ, the Son of the Living God.'

Jesus responded, '. . . on this rock, I will build My Church, and the powers of death shall not prevail against it' (Matthew 16:16, 18).

The Church is the people who have believed in Jesus Christ, and have received Him as Lord and Saviour. That is the rock on which the Church is built.

Although Peter and the disciples did believe in Jesus the Messiah, they were weak in their faith. When Jesus was crucified, most of the disciples fled. Even Peter denied that he knew Jesus. It was only after the resurrection of Jesus the Messiah, and the Mighty pouring out of the Spirit of God upon the disciples on the day of Pentecost, that they became bold and certain witnesses to the Gospel. When they were filled with the Spirit of God, they had power to witness and become the kind of people Jesus intended, when He said that the powers of death cannot stand against the Church.

The Church is the people who believe in Jesus Christ. The Church is not a building, although we sometimes do refer to the place in which Christians worship as a church. But in the New

Testament, Church never refers to a building. In fact, for many generations the early Christians did not meet in any special building for worship. They met in homes. In many places even today, the Christians worship in the homes of believers or even under a shady tree! The people who believe in Jesus, they are the Christian Church. These Christian believers should meet together regularly in the name of Jesus Christ. Christians in fellowship are the Church.

Jesus said, 'For where two or three are gathered in My name, there am I in the midst of them' (Matthew 18:20).

Jesus, the glorified Messiah, is present in the midst of believers through the presence of the Holy Spirit. Whenever believers meet together in the name of Jesus Christ, they sense that He is present among them. They pray in Jesus' name. Their prayers are answered. They confess their sins, and experience within their spirits that they are truly forgiven. They ask for guidance, and sense the guiding wisdom of the Lord. They seek for strength, and find renewal, refreshment, power, peace, grace, and love. They know that Jesus is indeed present in their midst as they meet together in His name.

After meeting, the Christians scatter to continue their normal work, teaching, farming, business, or whatever it is. Then again, perhaps a day later, or a week later, they come together in the name of Jesus. Again they sense that He is present in their midst. They are the Church: those who meet in the name of Jesus and then scatter into the world. The Church is the people who gather in Jesus' name and then scatter. The gathering and scattering community of Christian faith, they are the Church.

### Leadership in the Church

The Church has leaders and organization. The leadership plan for the Church has its beginnings with Jesus and His disciples. After the death and resurrection of the Messiah, his closest associates were called by God to become apostles and leaders of the Church. Soon the apostles needed administrative help to handle financial matters, especially in relationship to the poor widows in the Jerusalem Church. Under the guidance of the Holy Spirit, seven men were selected as apostolic assistants. They were ordained to their office, by the apostles laying hands on them, and praying for them (Acts 6:1–6). Later these apostolic assistants were called deacons. As congregations of Christians began to multiply, each local congregation also needed leaders. These local leaders were selected, under the guidance of the Holy Spirit, after prayer and fasting. They were called elders, and were also ordained by the laying on of hands by the apostles (Acts 14:23).

As the apostles grew older, or as the Church became too large for them to give it sufficient leadership, bishops were chosen and ordained. As the apostles left the scene, bishops replaced them as the overall leaders of the Church (2 Timothy 1:6-7). Thus we see that from the beginning, the Church developed a three-office ministry: bishops, deacons to assist the bishops, and elders for the leadership of local congregations. All were ordained by the laying on of hands by the leaders of the Church.

Today most Christian churches have a form of leadership which is somewhat similar to that which the early apostolic Church developed. Of course, there is considerable variation, but the general pattern of ordained leadership is practised in most churches. This simple, but effective, organization aids the Church greatly in doing its work in the world.

## Culture and the Church

As the Church grew, it began to experience considerable cultural differences within its fellowship. For example, the Jewish Christians practised circumcision, but Gentiles did not circumcise. Gentiles and Jews dressed differently too, and the food they ate was certainly not similar. The Church was perplexed. Should all Christians have the same cultural practices? In the Old Testament, the people of the covenant did belong to the same culture. Was this also necessary in the new covenant? Circumcision was particularly difficult, because in the Old Testament circumcision was the sign that a man was a member of the covenant community.

This issue finally led to a great conference, which was held in Jerusalem about A.D. 43. The Apostles and other Church leaders studied what the Old Testament said about the creation of the Church through the power of the Spirit, and they also listened to reports of what the Holy Spirit was doing in the lives of Gentile Christians who had become righteous people, after receiving the gift of the Spirit of God. Finally the Church decided that the Gentile Christians should be free to remain in their culture after becoming Christians. They did not have to follow Jewish or Old Testament dietary regulations or practices such as circumcision. However, they were to refrain from evil such as sexual immorality, or certain practices associated with idol worship (Acts 15:1–35).

This decision of the Jerusalem Conference is very significant, for it determined for ever that the Christian Church shall have cultural diversity. Wherever the Gospel goes, people are invited to accept the good news of salvation through Christ, and then put the Gospel to practice in their own local situation. They are to clothe their Christian experience in their own cultural clothing. It is for this reason that the Christian Church has more cultural diversity than any other religious community on earth. Christians in every society are free to remain in their culture as believers in Jesus Christ.

Nevertheless, Christians also experience an amazing unity The Bible says, 'There is one body and one Spirit, just as you were called to the one hope that belongs to your call, one Lord, one faith, one baptism, one God and Father of us all, Who is above all and through all in and all' (Ephesians 4:4–6). The unity of the Church makes it possible for Christians to experience brother-hood and oneness, even though they are culturally diverse. The Scriptures say, 'There is neither Jew nor Greek, there is neither slave nor free, there is neither male nor female; for you are all one in Christ Jesus '(Galatians 3:28).

### Diversity and co-operation in the Church

Sometimes diversity has led to misunderstandings between Christians. Occasionally differences have even led to the formation of particular Christian groups within the world-wide Church. This is one cause for the formation of Christian denominations. For example, one reason for the development of the Anglican Church in England during the sixteenth century was the desire of the English people to have a national church which would affirm desirable aspects of English culture. This church was formed more for cultural and national reasons than for doctrinal or theological reasons. In a similar manner, some modern 'in-dependent' African churches have formed because of a desire to make Christianity more African. Many times denominations have developed because of the good and Biblical desire to permit the Gospel to flourish and grow within a particular culture.

Nevertheless, it is not always that way. Sometimes Christians have divided because of a serious difference of opinion about what Christians should believe or practise. One such division is the separation between the Catholic Church and the Protestant Churches. We do not have space to go deeply into the reasons for that sixteenth century division. Yet we should mention that one of the main issues was different attitudes towards the Bible. Protestants believe that the Bible should be the only basis of authority in the Church. Catholics felt that the witness of the Holy Spirit through the Church's traditions and leadership is also important. These different viewpoints, concerning the basis for authority in the Church, helped to contribute to the division between the Catholic and Protestant Church about 450 years ago. The Protestant Church has also divided into denominations because of cultural or theological diversity.

Christians are aware that cultural diversity is right. Healthy Christian experience and commitment encourages variety. At the same time Christians are painfully aware that divisions in the Church which prevent good fellowship among Christians are sinful. They know that such divisions are evidence that Christians do not have sufficient love for one another. They confess the sin of division. In our modern day, we are finding that sometimes the Holy Spirit is helping to unite divided Christians in fellowship, as brothers and sisters in Jesus Christ. They are finding that the love of God helps them to overcome many of their differences. They are able to work together in a spirit of Christian love and co-operation, even though they might disagree on some things.

In some countries, councils of churches have been formed to help Christians express love and co-operation towards one another. There are also world Christian fellowships, such as the World Council of Churches or the World Evangelical Fellowship, which help Christians work together in a better way. All over the world today Christians are recognizing the sin of their divisions, and are trying to hear the voice of the Holy Spirit as they attempt to express love towards one another.

Many millions of Christians desire to experience more fully the love which Christ prayed for just before his crucifixion when He asked '. . . that they may become perfectly one . . .' (John 17:23). We are not yet perfectly one! Yet the Spirit of God is working among Christians in many parts of the world today. He is helping them to accept both variety and unity in Christ.

## A MUSLIM RESPONSE

The *Umma*, like the Church, is not a building. It is a community of believers. While the Church is people who have believed in Jesus Christ, received him as Lord and Saviour, the *Umma* is that community which entirely submits to Allah and takes instruction from His Seal of Prophets (PBUH). Leadership in the Church is not comparable to that of the *Umma*. The *Umma* has no ordained leaders after the fashion of the Church. In the *Umma*, it is God's Word (Qur'an), the *Sunnah* (practice) of Prophet Muhammad (PBUH), and the *Shari'a* (God's Divine Laws) that are the guiding principles of the *Umma*.

While appreciating that the Church has accepted cultural diversity, we learn that at times this has led to misunderstanding among Christians, even occasionally causing divisions in the Church. In contrast, Islam has come up with a single universal Islamic culture, generally common to the entire *Umma*. Although there is some diversity in the *Umma*, ideally the *Umma* surpasses ethnic, national, linguistic, and racial boundaries. It is for this reason that Muslims cannot talk of African, Turkish, Chinese, or American Islam. Perhaps it is for similar reasons that the *Umma* has not experienced so many divisions as characterize the Church today.

*'God is spirit, and those who worship Him must worship in spirit and truth'* (John 4:24).

# 22. Worship and Fellowship

## THE CHRISTIAN PRACTICE

If you live near Christians, you will notice that at least once a week they gather together in a home, under a tree, in a hall, or a church building for worship. The place in which Christians worship is not important. The significant aspect of Christian worship is the gathering together of believers, who worship the one true God Who has revealed Himself as Father, Son, and Holy Spirit. This is to say that all true Christian worship recognizes God as Father, Saviour, and Spirit Who is present with us now. Christians recognize the triune nature of God in worship. This is evident whenever you hear Christians pray. They pray to God the loving heavenly Father, in the name of Jesus the beloved Son Who has revealed God's redemptive love to mankind, and in the power of the Holy Spirit Who is the presence of God in the life of the believers. It is this Christian experience of the triune nature of God which is common to all Christian worship everywhere.

Otherwise there is no real commonality in Christian worship. Remember that at the Jerusalem Conference in A.D. 43, the Church decided that cultural diversity is right. Ever since that time, Christian worship has reflected considerable differences. Some Christians pray with a loud voice with everyone praying at the same time. Others have only the leader of the congregation leading in the prayers. Some stand when they pray, and others kneel. Some have a cross at the front of the Church, or candles lit, but others feel that these signs are not helpful, and have no such symbols in their churches. For some Christians rituals are very important, but for others the preaching of the Word of God is the most significant aspect of worship. Christian worship practices have great diversity, but all are united in grateful celebration of the love of God our Father, which has been revealed to us through Jesus Christ, and which is present with us now through the Holy Spirit.

Although Christians have great diversity in worship, there are several practices which are quite common. We shall mention a few.

## Baptism

Before Jesus was received into heaven, He commanded His disciples to go into all the world and 'make disciples of all nations, baptizing them in the name of the Father and of the Son and of the Holy Spirit, teaching them to observe all that I have commanded you· . . .' (Matthew 28:19,20). The disciples began to obey this command on the day of Pentecost, when they proclaimed the Gospel and about 3000 people entered the Church through believing in Jesus the Messiah and receiving baptism (Acts 2:37–42). The act of believing and the baptism seemed to go together. Ever since that Pentecost day, nearly 2000 years ago, baptism is performed for believers who are accepted as members of the Church.

Baptism is a ceremony involving: (1) confessing one's faith in Christ before God in the presence of witnesses, (2) receiving baptism with water in the name of the Father, the Son and the Holy Spirit. In some churches infants are baptized, in which case the parents or guardians symbolically make the confession of faith on behalf of the child; the baptism of infants is a sign that innocent children are also members of the covenant community. In all churches, water is used as a sign of cleansing, of the fullness of the Spirit, and of acceptance into the Church. In some churches only a few drops of water are sprinkled on the head, in other Christian communities handfuls of water are used, and in still others the candidate for membership is placed under the water as a sign that his sins are buried; the candidate rising out of the water after the baptism is a sign of rising with Christ to new and eternal life.

Some Christian groups baptize a person almost immediately after he confesses faith in Jesus Christ, but most churches have a period of instruction before the new believer can be accepted for baptism. This time of catechetical instruction is for two reasons: (1) to teach the new believer the doctrines and practices of the Church, (2) to have a period of time to see whether the new believer has experienced a change in conduct. Christians are to live righteously, and most churches require a period of time to know whether the new candidate for baptism has really experienced a change of life and conduct. After the completion of catechetical instruction, a public baptismal service is held.

In churches which baptize infants, the practice is somewhat different. In these churches the young person, who has been baptized as an infant, is invited to participate in confirmation classes, when he or she is about twelve years of age. These classes are similar to the catechetical classes which a new believer has to have before baptism. After the Church leaders are satisfied that the candidate for confirmation is a committed Christian, and that he or she understands the doctrines and practices of the Church, a confirmation service is held, in which those who have been baptized as infants are welcomed into the Church as full members and are admitted for the eucharist.

## Sunday worship

Christians should meet together for worship and fellowship regularly. Some Christians meet together daily. Many meet at least once a week. Normally the weekly meeting of Christians takes place on Sunday morning. This is because Jesus the Messiah rose from the dead on Sunday morning. The meeting of Christians on Sunday is a celebration and remembrance of the resurrection of Jesus.

The Church service on Sunday mornings varies greatly from group to group. But in all Christian communities, the central aspect of worship is the confession, and celebration, in thanksgiving for salvation through Jesus Christ whom God sent into the world. In most churches the reading of the Bible is an important aspect of the worship service. Also hymns are sung and prayers offered. Usually there is a sermon when the Gospel is proclaimed. Many churches also celebrate the eucharist or communion in the Sunday morning worship service.

## The eucharist

The eucharist (communion or mass) is a remembrance of the death and resurrection of Jesus Christ. The Old Testament Passover festival helps us to understand the meaning of the eucharist (Exodus 12). At the time when God delivered the Hebrew peoples from slavery under Pharaoh, He commanded each family to sacrifice a perfect lamb only one year old. The blood of the sacrificed lamb was placed on the two doorposts and lintel of the entrance to the home. Then the family met together inside the home and ate the roasted flesh of the sacrificed lamb to give them strength for their journey. While the Hebrew families were in their homes eating the roasted lamb the angel of God passed through the land of Pharaoh and slew the oldest child in every home which did not have blood over the entrance. When the people of the land saw what had happened, they begged the Hebrews to leave. In Hebrew history this great event is called the Passover, because the angel of death passed over every house which had blood over the door.

In thanksgiving for what God had done for them, every year at Passover time the Hebrew people would remember in a special way the manner in which God had saved them from slavery and death. They recognized that the perfect lamb which they had sacrificed was a sign of salvation.

Jesus was crucified at Passover time. The night of His crucifixion He ate the Passover meal with His disciples. During that supper together He took bread and broke it saying, 'Take, eat; this is My body'. Then He took a cup of wine and in a similar manner gave it to them saying,

> Drink of it, all of you; for this is My blood of the covenant, which is poured out for many for the forgiveness of sins. I tell you I shall not drink again of this fruit of the vine until that day when I drink it new with you in My Father's kingdom (Matthew 26:26–29).

This was the first eucharist or communion service. It was introduced by Jesus the Messiah Himself.

In the Christian Church, the eucharist is celebrated rather than the Passover because it was at the Passover feast that Jesus introduced the eucharist. In fact, Christians believe that the Old Testament Passover feast is a sign preparing people to understand and accept the crucifixion of Jesus as the perfect sacrifice for sin. The Passover was a sign pointing forward to the future sacrifice of Jesus on the cross.

The bread is a sign of the body of Christ, and the wine a sign of His blood which was given for our salvation and forgiveness when He gave Himself for our redemption on the cross.

The eucharist is also a sign of unity. Jesus shared one cup and broke one bread with His disciples. In the eucharist, the whole congregation drink and eat together from one cup and common bread. In this way the Church experiences a renewal of unity within the Christian fellowship. The eucharist is a profound celebration of unity in Christ.

The eucharist also reveals reconciliation between God and man. The material emblems of the eucharist are signs of the redemptive presence of God among men. The material and the spiritual dimensions of life are united in the eucharist. The eucharist is a sign that man, the creature, is invited to receive Divine grace. It is a sign of eating, of fellowship, of communion with God, our loving heavenly Father.

## Service

Service is also a dimension of Christian worship. The marvellous gift of salvation, the recreating grace of God, the experience of the redemptive love of God, the presence of the Holy Spirit in the life of the believer, releases the disciple of the Messiah to serve freely and joyously. The Bible says, 'I appeal to you therefore, brethren, by the mercies of God, to present your bodies as a living sacrifice, holy and acceptable to God, which is your spiritual worship '(Romans 12:1).

True worship includes offering ourselves in sacrificial service to our fellowmen. As a sign of self-giving service, most Christian congregations include the collection of money to be used in service to others as part of their worship expression. The giving of money in the worship experience is a sign that because God has redeemed us we also offer ourselves for others.

We have mentioned several significant aspects of Christian worship. All are important. Some Christians appreciate one aspect more greatly than other aspects. For example, many Protestants consider preaching to be the central event in Christian worship. Other Protestants believe that the central worship event is the fellowship with other believers. Catholics, especially, believe that the eucharist or mass is the central event. Still other groups may consider singing and rejoicing to be central, while others give prominence to praying for the sick and casting out evil spirits in the name of the risen glorified Messiah. These differences in emphasis do affect the manner in which the worship services are conducted. For example, Protestant churches tend to have very good sermons, while Catholic churches excel in beautiful communion ritual.

Yet the differences in worship practices should not obscure the one central event in all Christian fellowship. The meeting of Christians for worship is an expression and celebration of the unity and love of God. Christian worship is a participation, with thankfulness, in God's saving redemptive love. It is for this reason that whenever Christians meet for worship, they sense that the promise of Jesus is true indeed: 'Where two or three (or more) are gathered in My name, there am I in the midst of them' (Matthew 18:20). Through the presence of the Spirit of God within the worshipping congregation, Christians experience Jesus the Christ in their midst.

## A MUSLIM RESPONSE

The Christian practice of worship is quite different from the Muslim practice. It is the Christian experience of the triune nature of God in worship, which is common to all Christian worship everywhere; otherwise there is no real commonality in Christian worship. The person of Jesus Christ is central in Christian worship.

For Muslims, worship is a wide term which is applied beyond prayer (*salat*). Worship (*ibadah*) is the submission that Allah is your Master and you are His servant, and so all that the servant does in obedience to Him is *ibadah*. Every good deed performed to seek the pleasure of Allah is worship. This can be an individual act, or a collective one. There are some rituals of *ibadah* which have been made compulsory, and if left out, one commits a sin or ceases to be a Muslim.

The most important duty of *ibadah*, after acknowledging the oneness of Allah, is the *salat*. The Muslim prayer, whether congregational or individual, unlike the Christian form of worship, is uniform all over the world. The ranks of the faithful, their unison in movement behind the *imam* (leader of prayer), facing the direction of the Qibla, the *raka'h* (unit) and the *sujud* (prostration), which brings down the believer to the earth, is all performed in the same way. There is commonality in the language of the prayer, and in almost every detail.

Prayer, which is the centre of worship in Islam, is to none other than the Almighty Allah. Prayer is to be offered direct to Allah, and not through any intercessor.

*'For the kingdom of God does not mean food and drink but righteousness and peace and joy in the Holy Spirit'* (Romans 14:17).

# 23. Right Conduct

## THE CHRISTIAN IDEAL

The Christian Church does not have any organized system of universal law for right conduct. Although sometimes in Christian history some groups have tried to make a systematic law for conduct, this has never been acceptable to the Church as a whole. The reason Christians do not rely on a system of law to regulate their conduct is threefold:

1. Jesus the Messiah taught, 'You shall love the Lord your God with all your heart, and with all your soul, and with all your mind. This is the great and first commandment. And the second is like it, you shall love your neighbour as yourself. On these two commandments depend all the law and the prophets' (Matthew 22:37–40). Love is the key to all Christian morality. True love for one's neighbour can only come from the heart. It cannot be reduced to a set of rules. It is the inner attitude which is significant. That is the basis of Christian conduct; love for our fellowmen.

2. The Holy Spirit is present within us to guide us in the way of righteousness. Before Jesus was crucified, He promised that after He is received into heaven, God will send the Holy Spirit Who '. . . will guide you into all the truth; . . .' (John 16:13). Jesus also promised that the Holy Spirit will '. . . convince the world of sin and of righteousness and of judgement; . . .' (John 16:8). The Holy Spirit is the personal presence of God within the experience of the Christian believer and the Church. The Holy Spirit guides the believer and the Church in truth and righteousness. It is impossible to reduce into a formal ethical code this kind of personal encounter with God Who is the altogether righteous One. Christian righteousness springs from a fellowship relationship with God. It cannot be codified. It is too personal for that.

3. The presence of the Holy Spirit in the life of the Christian recreates the image of God which was spoiled when man turned away from God. It is the recreation in righteousness of the person that God is interested in. Slavish obedience to laws does not recreate the person. He can still think evil thoughts even though outwardly he might look like a righteous person. Jesus was supremely concerned about the inner man because that is where righteousness or evil originate. It is for this reason that Jesus berated the hypocrisy of the religious leaders of His day saying:

Woe to you, scribes and pharisees, hypocrites! For you cleanse the outside of the cup and of the plate, but inside they are full of extortion and rapacity. You blind Pharisee! First cleanse the inside of the cup and of the plate, that the outside also may be clean (Matthew 23:25, 26).

Throughout the New Testament there is a tremendous emphasis on the need to be transformed, to be recreated, to become like Christ within the inner person. The Apostle Paul has written under the inspiration of the Holy Spirit,

Put off your old nature which belongs to your former manner of life and is corrupt through deceitful lusts, and be renewed in the spirit of your minds, and put on the new nature, created after the likeness of God in true righteousness and holiness (Ephesians 4:22-24).

The recreated person, who is living under the guidance of the Holy Spirit, does need principles which help him to measure whether he is indeed living in 'the likeness of God in true righteousness and holiness.' What are the principles of righteousness which the Holy Spirit has revealed through the prophets in the past? What are the principles of righteousness which Jesus the Messiah has taught? What are the characteristics of the truth which the Holy Spirit reveals to the people of the covenant today? We shall examine the answers to those questions by looking briefly at some of the basic moral teachings which have been revealed to us through both the Prophet Moses and the life and teachings of Jesus the Messiah.

Much of the Torah consists of teachings on right conduct and worship, which God revealed to the Prophet Moses. All of these principles for right conduct are summarized in the Ten Commandments which God revealed to the People of the Covenant at Mount Sinai (Exodus 20:1–17).

A summary of these commandments is as follows:

1. You shall have no other gods except the one true God.
2. You shall not make for yourself an image.
3. You shall not use the name of the Lord your God in a careless manner.
4. Remember the seventh day of the week, and keep it holy.
5. Honour your father and your mother.
6. You shall not kill.
7. You shall not commit adultery.
8. You shall not steal.
9. You shall not tell a lie against your neighbour.
10. You shall not covet anything that belongs to your neighbour.

Christians everywhere recognize that these Ten Commandments are right. All Christians should abide by principles revealed in the Ten Commandments. They are basesd on the principle of love of God and one's fellowman.

Elsewhere in the Torah, God revealed that we should love God and our neighbour (Deuteronomy 6:4, Leviticus 19:18). When Jesus the Messiah appeared, He pointed out that the commandment to love is the greatest commandment of all, and that all the other commandments in the Bible are summarized in the law of love. Jesus said that on these commandments to love '. . . depend all the law and the prophets' (Matthew 22:40). It is for this reason that Jesus commanded his disciples, '. . . love one another. . .' (John 15:12). Through His life and teachings, Jesus the Messiah taught people the meaning of love. In the previous chapter, we have already mentioned how Jesus served people by healing them and caring for their needs. He welcomed and forgave sinners. The forgiveness He expressed at His crucifixion is the supreme revelation of love. However, it is not only His deeds which reveal love. His teachings are also helpful.

On one occasion Jesus took His disciples onto a mountain near the Sea of Galilee, and taught them moral principles based on love. He explained to them that true righteousness depends on an inner spiritual commitment to God. These teachings are called the Sermon on the Mount, and they are recorded in Matthew chapters 5, 6, 7.

Jesus the Messiah began the Sermon on the Mount by saying, 'Blessed are the poor in spirit for theirs is the Kingdom of heaven' (Matthew 5:3). Christians believe that the Kingdom is '... righteousness and peace and joy in the Holy Spirit' (Romans 14:17). Jesus said that the 'poor' in spirit enter or inherit this Kingdom. It is only those who recognize that they are sinful, who recognize that they are not living in right fellowship with God who seek forgiveness it is only these 'poor' people who experience God's saving grace. It is the 'poor in spirit', who are willing to receive salvation through Jesus the Messiah. It is these needy people who open their lives to the recreating power of the Holy Spirit. It is they who enter the Kingdom of Heaven.

These 'poor in spirit' people experience an inner recreation of attitudes which affects all their relationships. Jesus gave specific examples of the change of attitude which people should experience who have entered the Kingdom of Heaven. Here are several examples of what He said:

*Peace* (Matthew 5:21–26).
In the Ten Commandments we read, 'You shall not kill.' But Jesus the Messiah taught that hate is also wrong. It is hate which drives people to kill. We need to become free of evil attitudes towards other people. Jesus said, 'I say to you that everyone who is angry with his brother shall be (in danger of) judgement...' (Matthew 5:22).

*Marriage* (Matthew 5:27–32),
One of the Ten Commandments says, 'You shall not commit adultery' (Exodus 20:14). But Jesus the Messiah said that any desire for a woman who is not one's wife is sin. He said, 'I say unto you that everyone who looks at a woman lustfully has already committed adultery with her in his heart' (Matthew 5:28). Adultery destroys marriage and it also destroys the person. It is a terrible evil. For this reason Jesus said that if any part of our body such as the eye tempts us into sin, it is better to have the eye plucked out than to yield to the temptation. 'It is better that you lose one of your members, than that your whole body go into hell' (Matthew 5:29).

Jesus also taught that divorce is wrong. 'I say to you that everyone who divorces his wife, except on the ground of unchastity, makes her an adulteress and whoever marries a divorced woman commits adultery' (Matthew 5:32). Divorce is evil because it breaks the marriage unity which God has planned. When God created Adam and Eve we read that they became 'one flesh' (Genesis 2:24). The one flesh unity of marriage is a miracle of God's grace. Divorce spoils and destroys the sacred gift of 'one flesh' unity in marriage. Jesus commanded, 'What therefore God has joined together, let no man separate' (Matthew 19:6). Jesus said that, although it is true that in the old covenant people were permitted to divorce, this was only permitted because the 'hardness' of people's hearts (Matthew 19:8). Divorce should never take place among new covenant people, where the Holy Spirit is present in the life of the believer and the Church creating true righteousness (Matthew 5:33-37).

Although the Bible never specifically prohibits polygamy, nevertheless, most Christian churches do not permit the practise of polygamy among their members. Although some men of God in the Old Testament had more than one wife, none of those polygamous marriages is ever described in the Bible as ideal; in fact, most are described as being sadly unhappy. Polygamy spoils the 'one flesh' union of marriage. One flesh unity demands total loyalty to one's marriage partner. For a woman to have several husbands, or a man to have several wives, spoils that deep inner meaning of marriage as one flesh union, in which the husband is called to love his wife as his own body, and the wife is called to respect her husband deeply. In fact the Bible commands the husband to give himself in suffering sacrificial love for his wife just as Christ has given Himself in suffering sacrificial love for the Church (Ephesians 5:21–33).

### Truthfulness (Matthew 5:33–37).

The ninth commandment says, 'You shall not bear false witness' (Exodus 20:16). Jesus the Messiah pointed out that the inner meaning of this command is that we should not even swear, because the person who swears seems to be saying that sometimes he can tell a lie; he is really truthful only when he swears. The truthful person never has to swear, because his word is always true. The truthful man only needs to say 'yes' or 'no' and his associates will know that he has told the truth.

### Forgiveness (Matthew 5:38–48).

We have mentioned several times that Jesus taught that the greatest commandment is to love God, and the second greatest is to love one's neighbour as oneself. Jesus the Messiah taught that the law of love demands that we forgive our enemy. Although, some teachers have said, 'An eye for an eye and a tooth for a tooth' Jesus taught, '...love your enemies and pray for those who persecute you,...' (Matthew 5:28, 44). He was very specific, saying that if someone takes our coats, we should give him our shirts as well, and if someone slaps us on one cheek, we should turn the other cheek. If our enemy deserves punishment, that is up to God; it is not our responsibility to do evil to our enemy. (Romans 12:19).

Hate and violence creates more hate and violence. Taking revenge against our enemy does not erase the hate between us. Only forgiveness can heal the violence. Only love can destroy the hate. If our enemy knows that we love him, he might become our friend, but if we use violence, we shall both be hurt and the hate between us will increase.

## *Riches* (Matthew 6:19–34).

The last of the Ten Commandments says that we should not covet anything which our neighbour has. Coveteousness is the evil desire to take that which someone else possesses. It is our desire for riches and things which is the root of coveteousness. Jesus taught us to avoid putting any trust in riches or possessions. The Christian is to seek for righteousness; he is to seek first for the Kingdom of God. When we love God most of all, He will take care of all our other needs. Jesus said,

> Therefore do not be anxious, saying, 'What shall we eat?' or 'What shall we wear?' ... But seek first his kingdom and His righteousness, and all these things shall be yours as well (Matthew 6:31, 33).

Jesus has much more to say about the way of righteousness which we cannot comment on in this short chapter. Probably the most astonishing part of His sermon was when He said, 'You, therefore, must be perfect as your heavenly Father is perfect' (Matthew 5:48)! How can we live as righteously as God? Certainly that kind of righteousness is only possible as the Holy Spirit recreates our lives into the true image and likeness of God. And as Jesus said, we can only experience that kind of recreation when we become poor in spirit, when we confess our failure, our sin, our need for salvation.

'And when Jesus finished these sayings, the crowds were greatly surprised at His teaching, for He taught them as one who had authority, and not as their scribes' (Matthew 7:28–29).

Christian people are those who recognize the authority of Jesus the Messiah. They submit to God's will by acknowledging Jesus as Lord and Saviour. They are disciples (followers) of Jesus. The first Christians said that those who confessed 'Jesus is Lord', were walking in 'The Way' (Acts 18:26). Even today those who follow Jesus do walk in 'The Way'. This is 'The Way' of love, 'The Way' which Jesus the Messiah lived.

## A MUSLIM RESPONSE

The Christian Church, unlike the Muslim *Umma*, has no system of universal law for right conduct. It is the Christians' confessed view that love, which is central to their teaching, cannot be reduced to a set of rules. However, Muslims, who have both a universal Divine law, and a permanent scheme of revealed moral values, are of the view that man being imperfect, and having limited knowledge, must be guided at all times by this law and moral values. Although man is commanded to practise justice, he does not know how to go about it. So, the Divine law gives him every detail on how to practise justice and mercy at every instance.

On the other hand, the scheme of moral values on which Christian conduct is based is somewhat similar to that of Muslims, although love is made to supercede every other moral value in Christianity. This overstressing of 'love' in all aspects of the Christian life has at times, in Muslim eyes, rendered the Christian ideal of conduct more theoretical than practical.

One practical issue on which Christians and Muslims painfully differ is marriage and divorce. Marriage in Islam is a contract between a man and a woman which is concluded in God's name, and is therefore a sacred institution. Everything should be done to uphold this sacred contract.

However, if there are severe obstacles in marriage which cannot be overcome through reconciliation, then Islam, in its practical teachings, has permitted divorce (*talaq*). Divorce should only be a last resort. The Prophet Muhammad (PBUH) said: 'That of all things permitted by law, divorce is the most hateful in sight of God.'* Again the Qur'an advises: 'If women obey you, then

---

*Reported by Son of Omar, Abu Dawd and Hakim, *Fikqi Sunnah*, Vol. II, Beirut, by Sayid Sabiq, Daarul-Kitab-l-Araby, p. 241.

do not seek a way against them.'**Islam would not tolerate, unhappy, faithless, loveless, stagnant marriages. It is for this practical
reason that divorce is permitted.

In the same way, forgiveness is recommended as a high moral
virtue of Islam, but it must be given in a practical manner. In
Islam a wronged or oppressed person has the freedom to resist
and retaliate by bringing the offender to book or dealing some
punishment to him. He has also the right to forgive the offender,
entrusting Allah with the results of his actions. The Qur'an states:

> The recompense of an evil deed is punishment proportionate
> to it, but whoever forgives (the injury caused him thereby)
> and makes reconciliation, he shall have his reward from
> Allah. Surely God does not love the wrong doer (Qur'an
> 42:40).

Another verse says: 'Praised are they who restrain their anger
and pardon the faults of others; and God loves those who do good
to others' (Qur'an 3:134).

Practically in Islam, there is neither the extreme of an eye for
an eye, nor the opposite one of turning the left cheek when the
right is smitten. There is no giving away the trousers to the
brother who has taken away the shirt!

---

**Qur'an 4:34.

*'And He [the Messiah] said to them, "Go into all the world and preach the Gospel to the whole creation"'* (Mark 16:15).

# 24. The Mission of the Church

## THE WORK OF THE CHURCH

Jesus the Messiah began His ministry by proclaiming in the synagogue in Nazareth that the Spirit of the Lord was upon Him to preach good news to the poor, to proclaim freedom to the captives, to give sight to the blind and liberty to the oppressed (Luke 4:18). This is the announcement that the Kingdom of God has begun; in Jesus the Messiah the will of God was perfectly extended into human history. Jesus lived the Kingdom; He was the Kingdom. People who responded to him in faith received healing in every way: sins were forgiven, the lame walked, the blind saw, the poor received hope. The Messiah is the breakthrough of the Kingdom of God into history.

The Church is the community of faith which continues that work of God which Jesus began (1 Corinthians 12,13). The Church is a continuing sign among the nations that the Kingdom of God has begun. Through the presence of the Holy Spirit in the life of the Church, the Kingdom of God keeps on breaking into our communities and our lives. The Church is a sign, a witness in the world that salvation is at hand.

The mission of the Church flows out of the experience of redemptive love. Redeemed people are compelled by the love of God to share His Love with their fellowmen. The overflowing love of God in the experience of the Church gives Christians a profound urge to serve their fellowmen, with the same spirit of self-giving love which they have experienced through Jesus the Messiah. Christians desire to '. . . walk in love, as Christ loved us and gave Himself up for us, . . .' (Ephesians 5:2). It is love for others which is at the centre of true Christian mission.

How does the Church give witness to the presence of the Kingdom of God? How does it share God's love with the world? How does it reveal to the world that, through Jesus the Messiah, God's eternal reign has begun? How does it become a sign to the nations that the redemptive love of God is present, that God's good purpose for history will triumph.

There are three principal ways in which the Church performs mission.

*First, the Church performs its mission through fellowship.* Those who are members of the Church are called by God to love one another (1 Corinthians 13). Love was remarkably present at Pentecost, when the Church was created. Believers actually sold their possessions and gave all that they had to the poor! We read,

> And all who believed were together and had all things in common; and they sold their possessions and goods and distributed them to all, as any had need. And day by day, attending the temple together and breaking bread in their homes, they partook of food with glad and generous hearts, praising God and having favour with all the people (Acts 2:44–47).

Pentecost was an unusual expression of love. Yet wherever the Church is truly faithful, Christians do express love towards one another. Most Christian congregations have ways in which to share with any believer who suffers misfortune. If a member's house burns down, the believers will take an offering and probably help to rebuild the home which has been destroyed. In countless ways Christians in the local congregation attempt to show love to one another. They obey the Biblical command, '. . . let us do good to all men, and especially to those who are of the household of faith, (Galatians 6:10).

Not only is love expressed within the local church. Christians also attempt to show love to their brothers and sisters in other parts of the world. This is because each local church is part of the universal Christian Church. We have already mentioned how world wide councils and fellowships represent ways in which Christians attempt to express their unity and love. These channels of fellowship flow in many different directions. Each Christian denomination is also a fellowship, which normally unites Christians of different nations together within a particular denominational family. Whatever the case may be, the Church not only expresses Christian fellowship within the local situation, but also attempts to express Christian love across national boundaries. This international fellowship is evident for example, in the flow of financial assistance from one Christian fellowship to another which has experienced a misfortune such a drought. Another example is hospitality. Whenever we travel to foreign countries we find that our Christian brothers and sisters in the foreign country offer us hospitality, even though we are complete strangers. Christian love unites even strangers in fellowship.

Fellowship is the first dimension of Christian mission in the world. It is the love which Christians have for each other, which more than any other aspect of Christian mission, is a witness that the Kingdom of God has come. Jesus said, 'By this all men will know that you are my disciples, if you have love for one another' (John 13:35).

*Second, the Church performs its mission through service.* Perhaps there are Christian churches in your home community. What kinds of service do they perform in your community ? In thousands of communities around the world the Church is involved in a wide variety of social service ministries. On a world wide basis today some of these ministries include: refugee assistance, famine relief, medical ministries, educational development from the primary level up to university, desert control and tree planting, agricultural and livestock development, mental health, homes for the aged, housing development, home industries for low income families, adult literacy, road building, marriage counselling, ministries to delinquent children or to orphans, reading rooms and libraries, disaster reconstruction after floods or earthquakes, exploring new sources of energy, reconciliation when there is conflict between nations, ministry to lepers, trade schools, recreation centres—the list is inexhaustible. The Church is called by God to attempt to be a sign in the community and to the nations that God is concerned, that He does love, that He desires to save us from all that is evil.

Through these ministries of loving service, the Church continues the work which Jesus began when he proclaimed the presence of the Kingdom of God among people. The Church shares the redemptive love of God with others. The Church attempts to be a sign of the presence of God's Kingdom within history through its ministries of love and service. Wherever there is human need, the Church is called to minister, to serve, to express God's love in action.

The Church does not believe that it can solve all the problems of human need around the world. That is impossible. Societies everywhere experience rebellion against God. Evil is present. But the Church is called to be a sign of the Kingdom of God, a conscience within society.

An example from Kenya is helpful. Some years ago an employment problem developed for primary school graduates who could not go on to secondary school. The Church recognized the problem, and began several polytechnics to train primary students in basic technical skills for employment. This ministry was highly successful. Soon society as a whole recognized the value of polytechnics, and today the polytechnics are supported by the Government. There are countless examples of this. The Church in its ministries of social service is a conscience to society, helping to show the path toward more effective humanization. It is a sign of God's loving intention for mankind.

*Third, the Church performs its mission by proclaiming the Gospel throughout the World.* Before Jesus was received into heaven, He commanded His disciples,

> Go therefore and make disciples of all nations baptizing them in the name of the Father and of the Son and of the Holy Spirit, teaching them to observe all that I have commanded you; and lo, I am with you always, to the close of the age (Matthew 28:19,m 20).

He went on to say, 'But you shall receive power when the Holy Spirit has come upon you; and you shall be My witnesses in Jerusalem and in all Judea and Samaria and to end of earth' (Acts 1:8). God has commanded the Church to take the Gospel to the ends of the earth. Christians are commanded to preach with urgency calling on people to repent and believe in Jesus the Messiah as the Lord and Saviour Whom God has sent to redeem mankind. They are commanded to baptize and teach the nations forming new church fellowships among all peoples. Christians call this command the Great Commission.

After Pentecost, the Church began to obey the Great Commission. In the lifetime of the apostles, Christian missionaries took the Gospel from Palestine into lands hundreds and even thousands of miles from Jerusalem. Within half a century believers had been baptized and churches formed from India in the east to Spain in the west. Egypt and other parts of northern Africa had also received the Gospel.

Sometimes the Church has failed to continue the Great Commission, or the Church has failed to understand the Great Commission and has attempted to spread the Church through warfare and violence. For example, several communities in Europe were 'converted' through conquest by 'Christian' armies. Christians are saddened that during the Crusades in the Middle Ages

Christian armies conquered the Middle East and tried to forcefully convert peoples to Christianity. These are horrible examples of a tragic Christian failure to understand and practise the Great Commission.

At the same time, many periods in the history of the Church have been blessed by multitudes of faithful Christian missionaries, who gave their lives to take the Gospel to the ends of the earth. These days more missionaries are serving around the world than at any time in the history of the Christian Church. Recently the Presbyterian Church in Kenya sent a missionary to New York in the United States. Some Tanzanian Christians are sharing the Gospel in China. Japanese missionaries have gone to South America. Pakistani Christians are witnessing in Kuwait. Indian Christians are ministering in Sudan. Hungarian missionaries serve in Kenya. Christians move in all directions from their home Church community, from their local 'Jerusalem', and wherever they go they take the Gospel. Many of these witnesses are commissioned and sent by their own local congregation to go to a foreign country to proclaim the Gospel. Others go for business, professional, or educational reasons, but wherever they go they should share the Gospel.

Of course the Church must remember that proclaiming the Gospel needs to begin at home. Faithful Christian congregations attempt to share the Gospel with their neighbours first of all. That is always the beginning of mission. But repeatedly Christian congregations also sense the call of the Spirit of God to go beyond the immediate neighbourhood to peoples who have never heard the Gospel. The Bible reveals that it is God's will that every people on earth hear the Gospel before the end of history, and that fellowships of believers develop among these peoples (Matthew 24:14, 28:16–20; Acts 1:8; Philippians 2:9–11).

Christians believe that the Church is a sign of the Kingdom of God which broke into human history through Jesus Christ and the Pentecost event when the Holy Spirit was poured out upon the believers. They believe that the mission of the Church is to be a sign and witness among the nations of the presence of the Kingdom of God among men. As we have mentioned, the Church becomes a sign of the Kingdom by continuing the work and ministry which Jesus Christ began: this includes fellowship, service, and witness.

The witness of the Bible is that at the end of history Jesus the Messiah will return to earth in glory, and the Kingdom of God will be fulfilled. At that time the nations and peoples of the earth will be judged. Those who have persisted in their rebellion against God will experience eternal punishment. The earth will pass away and human history will be consummated. Those who have responded to God's grace and have begun to participate in the Kingdom of God will experience eternal salvation. God's reign will be consummated. The Kingdom of God which has begun through the first coming of Jesus the Messiah will be completed and fulfilled. All things in heaven and earth will acknowledge Jesus the Messiah as the One Whom God has appointed Lord and Saviour. That is God's plan for history (Mark 14:62; Philippians 2:9–11; Revelation 20:11–15, 21:1–8, 22–27).

## A MUSLIM RESPONSE

Both Muslims and Christians strive to proclaim 'good news' to the world, as commanded by God and exemplified by their respective Prophets. The two communities take service as a fundamental duty to humanity, and especially to the community of faith.

However, the two organize their missions differently. Islam, which has no ordained hierarchy of priesthood or organized missionary orders like Christianity, has been mostly propagated and spread by committed Muslim individuals who have had only limited means of livelihood. It is for this reason that Muslim service, through visible material structures like hospitals, roads, or conference centres, has been conspicuously lacking, especially in areas where Muslims are in the minority. Although Muslims stress preaching, this does not mean that they are only concerned about life in the hereafter. Islam, as a complete way of life, is naturally as much concerned about this life as the life after death. Work and service is a duty enjoined by God and is part of Muslim worship.

While Islam acknowledges the second coming of the Messiah, nevertheless, the nature of His anticipated mission is different from the Christian anticipation. Muslims believe that the Messiah will return to earth to firmly establish the true religion of Islam before the final judgement.

# Conclusion

Islam and Christianity are two living faiths which claim to have a mission to the whole of mankind. In this book we have highlighted, albeit briefly, some of the major issues which bring Muslims and Christians together or separate them completely in their worship of God and witness among their fellowmen.

We, the authors, are thankful for those beliefs we hold in common. We both recognize the faith of Abraham and seek to understand and live in accordance with the faith which he exercized. We believe that faith needs to be enlightened through the witness of prophets, apostles, and the Scriptures. We believe that revelation is not a human invention, but rather the gracious gift of God to man. We believe that history has meaning, that it is moving towards a consummation in judgement. We both believe in the resurrection of the dead. We believe that all this springs from God Who is the sovereign, transcendent, righteous Creator of all. Each of us believe that God commands His people to witness and invite unbelievers into repentance and into the community of faith. We believe that God has established a witnessing community of faith.

While giving thanks for and affirming the faith which unites us, we also confess that our respective witnesses differ in important ways. The Muslim witness is that the Qur'an is God's final and definitive revelation of His perfect will to mankind. The Christian witness is that Jesus the Messiah is the Living Word of God in human form. For the Muslim the Qur'an is the criterion of truth. For the Christian the total Biblical witness culminating in Jesus the Messiah is the criterion of truth. And all that a Muslim or a Christian believes about man, God, salvation, guidance, righteousness, revelation, judgement or community is determined by these respective commitments.

In our dialogue, we have sensed that there are areas in which our beliefs are complementary. We give thanks for these points of commonality. But at the same time we are aware of significant differences. Both Islam and Christianity agree that God is merciful, that He loves. The question is, how closely does God choose to identify with our human situation. That is the fundamental question: How does God express His love and mercy. In Islam, God's mercy is supremely expressed through the revelation of a perfect law. In Christian faith God's love is supremely expressed in the suffering, redemptive love revealed in the life, crucifixion, and resurrection of Jesus the Messiah. These are not superficial differences. They deal with the most fundamental questions of the meaning of human existence. There is no way that a Muslim and a Christian can honestly proclaim that these differences are irrelevant or insignificant.

The nature of the theological issue is so exceedingly profound that the questions at stake cannot be appropriately understood or resolved through propositional polemics or logical positivisms. Our conversation in the interest of truth must move on the level of ultimate reality, the reality which probes much more deeply into the meaning of human existence than mere rationalism is ever capable. On this we both agree: truth is the *Word* of authoritative revelation from God. That common starting point is both the point of convergence and divergence between us. Is the Word of revelation pre-eminently a Book or supremely evident in a Person? That issue cannot be resolved by argument; the very nature of the issue demands patience, listening, and witness by both communities of faith.

Nevertheless, we believe that the pain caused by these differences should not prevent us from continuing conversation. The issues which divide us must not build walls of hostility between us so that the dialogue ceases. If we truly desire truth, and a deeper understanding of one another, then our mutual conversation must continue. The conversation should move on many different levels. This book has been a written conversation. But there are also other levels of conversation which are equally important. Probably the most significant level of conversation should be good neighbourliness. We must learn to know one another as friends. We must pray to God asking Him to help us cultivate bridges of love between ourselves. We must learn the conversation of love, forgiveness, respect, good neighbourliness, listening, and witness.

Amen.

# Glossary

## Islamic terms

| | |
|---|---|
| *abd* | the servant or slave of God |
| Abdallah | Muhammad's (PBUH) father |
| Abu Bakr | one of the first Muslim believers and also the first Caliph |
| Abu Talib | Muhammad's (PBUH) uncle |
| Adam | the father of all people, the husband of Eve (Hauwa), who was the first woman |
| *adhan* | call to prayer |
| *Ahl al-Kitab* | People of the Book, that is Jews and Christians |
| *al-asma' al husna* | the ninety-nine beautiful names of God |
| Ali | one of the first Muslim believers and also cousin and son-in-law to the Prophet. He became the fourth Caliph |
| Amina | Muhammad's (PBUH) mother |
| *Ansar* | the helpers in Madinah |
| *aya* | a verse in the Qur'an |
| *Basmalah* | the praise statement which every Muslim must say before doing anything: 'In the Name of Allah, the Compassionate, the Merciful' (*Bis-mi-llahi ar-Rahamani ar-Rahim*). All Quranic *surahs* except one begin with the *Basmalah* |
| Battle at Badr | Muslims defeated the infidels |
| Bilal and Khabbab | Muslims who suffered severe persecution in Makkah |
| the Books of God | there are five books which God has sent down to man. The Book revealed through Abraham (*Suhuf*) has been lost. The other four have not been lost |
| *Din, al-.* | religion |
| *Fatiha, al-* | the opening chapter of the Qur'an, the perfect prayer for Muslims |
| *fuqaha* | Doctors of Islamic law |
| The Garden | a heavenly paradise above the earth where Adam and Hauwa were placed before they yielded to the temptation of *Iblis* |
| *ghusul* | bathing in the prescribed Muslim manner |

171

| | |
|---|---|
| *Hadith* | the written traditions concerning the prophet which include both his teachings and practices |
| *haj* | the pilgrimage to the Ka'bah |
| Hauwa | Eve, the mother of all people, the wife of Adam who was the first man |
| *Hafz* | Quranic memorizers |
| *Hijrah* | the migration from Makkah to Yathreb (Madinah), A.D. 622 The beginning of the Islamic era |
| *Hudaibiyya* | the treaty between the Makkan Quraish and the Muslim *Umma* |
| *ibadat* | devotional worship and submission |
| *Iblis* | Satan who is the source of all evil |
| *ihsan* | right conduct |
| *ijima* | consensus |
| *Imam* | the head of the Shi'a Muslims who traces his geneology to the Prophet |
| *imam* | the leader of prayers in the mosque. |
| *iman* | belief or faith |
| *isnad* | the chain of witness through which the *Hadith* has been transmitted |
| *iqra* | recite the recitation of Divine revelation |
| *jahiliyya* | the time of ignorance in Arabia before the coming of the Prophet Muhammad (PBUH) |
| *Jalil, al-* | Most Majestic; one of the names of God |
| *Janna* | Paradise. The place Adam and Hauwa first lived, and the place to which the true slaves of Allah will return |
| *Jibril* | Gabriel through whom God has sent down His Books to the apostles |
| *jihad* | striving in the path of Allah |
| *jinn* | a spirit. Some *jinns* are evil and some are good. The evil *jinns* are followers if *Iblis* |
| *Juma* | Friday congregational prayer |
| *Ka'bah* | the house of God in Makkah in which there is a sacred black stone towards which all Muslims face when they pray |
| Khadija | Muhammad's (PBUH) first wife |
| *khalifa* | Vicegerent. Man was sent by God to earth to be His *khalifa* or caretaker on |

| | |
|---|---|
| | earth in obedience to the Divine command |
| *kufr* | disbelief and atheism. One of the greatest sins in Islam |
| *Lat, al-* | the sun goddess in pre-Islamic Arabia, who was worshipped as one of the three daughters of Allah |
| *Lailat ul-Qadar* | the Night of Power when Muhammad (PBUH) received his first revelation |
| *Manat, al-* | the goddess of destiny in pre-Islamic Arabia, who was considered to be one of three daughters of Allah |
| *Mir'aj* | the ascension of the Prophet (PBUH) |
| Moses | the Prophet of God through whom the Torah was revealed |
| *mosque* | a building in which Muslims gather for prayer |
| Mount Hira | the place where Muhammad (PBUH) first began to receive revelation |
| *Muhajirun* | the emigrants to Madinah |
| *Munafiqun* | hypocrite Muslims |
| *nabbi* | a prophet of God who proclaims the will of God |
| Negus, King | Abyssinian Christian King who gave the Muslims refuge |
| *Qibla* | the direction of prayer |
| *qiyas* | analogical reasoning |
| *Quraish* | the tribe of the Prophet Muhammad (PBUH) |
| *Rahim* | Most Merciful; one of the names of God |
| *Rahman* | Most Gracious; one of the names of God |
| *Ramadhan* | the month of fasting |
| *rasul* | an apostle of God through whom God reveals a Book |
| *sahaba* | Companions of the Prophet Muhammad (PBUH) |
| *salah* | the ritual prayer in Islam |
| *saum* | fasting |
| *Shahada* | the Muslim credal witness: 'There is no god but Allah, and Muhammad is the Apostle of Allah.' |
| *Shari'a* | the Law of God |
| *Shi'a* | the Muslim community who believe that |

|                |                                                              |
|----------------|--------------------------------------------------------------|
|                | the head of the community should be a descendant of the Prophet |
| *shirk*        | associating Allah with other gods. The greatest sin in Islam |
| *Sunnah*       | the way or practices of the Prophet                          |
| *Sunni*        | the Muslim community who look to the Qur'an, *Sunnah* and community consensus for authority |
| *Surah*        | a chapter in the Qur'an                                       |
| *taharah*      | purification                                                 |
| *tanzil*       | the sending down of Books from heaven                        |
| *'ulama*       | scholars of Islamic law and theology                         |
| *'Umar*        | an early convert to Islam who later became the second Caliph |
| *Umma*         | the community of Islam                                       |
| *'Uthman*      | one of the first Muslim believers and also the third Caliph  |
| *Uzza, al-*    | the goddess Venus in pre-Islamic Arabia, who was considered to be one of the three daughters of Allah |
| *Wahay*        | Divine revelation                                            |
| *wudu*         | ablution before prayers                                      |
| *zakat*        | obligatory alms                                              |

# Christian terms

| | |
|---|---|
| apostles | leaders of the early Church |
| baptism | a sign with water that a person is accepted into the Christian Church |
| Bethlehem | the Judean town where Jesus was born |
| bishop | a Church leader responsible for a group of Christian congregations |
| Church | the gathered community who believe in Jesus the Messiah as Saviour and Lord |
| covenant | a solemn agreement between two or more persons. God has invited mankind into a covenant of blessing with Himself |
| deacon | a Church leader who assists the minister or bishop |
| El or Elohim | the name for God used by Abraham. El or Elohim is the Hebrew form of the Arabic name 'Allah' |
| eucharist or communion | the sharing of bread and wine as a sign of new life and communion experienced through the life, death, and resurrection of Jesus the Messiah |
| elder | a minister in the early Church |
| Epistles | letters written by apostles to churches |
| Gabriel | the angel who came to Mary before the birth of Jesus |
| Garden of Eden | the place where Adam and Eve first lived |
| Gospel | Good News (*Euaggellion* or *Injil*) that God has acted redemptively in Jesus the Messiah |
| Great Commission | the command of Jesus to His disciples to preach the Gospel in the whole world |
| Herod, King | King of Judea at the time when Jesus was born |
| I AM | the name for God which was revealed to the Prophet Moses at the burning bush |
| Immanuel | a name for the Messiah which means 'God with us' |
| incarnation | the belief that God has revealed Himself in Jesus the Messiah |
| Jerusalem | the city in which Jesus was crucified |

| | |
|---|---|
| Jerusalem Conference | a Christian conference held in A.D. 43 to discuss the Christian attitude towards culture |
| John the Baptist | the prophet who baptized and prepared people to receive the Messiah |
| Joseph | the man who was engaged to Mary at the time when she gave birth to Jesus. He became her husband |
| Joseph of Arimathea | a rich man who provided a grave for Jesus |
| Kingdom of God | the rule of God in heaven and earth |
| Messiah | 'The Anointed One'. The Semitic form of the Greek word 'Kristos' or 'Christ' |
| Mount Sinai | the place where God revealed the Ten Commandments |
| Nazareth | the Galilean town where Jesus grew up |
| New Testament | the portion of the Bible written after the coming of the Messiah |
| Old Testament | the portion of the Bible written before the coming of the Messiah |
| ordain | the manner in which Church leaders are commissioned to their task by the bishops or ministers laying hands on them and praying for the Holy Spirit to give the necessary gifts of leadership |
| Passover | the feast which reminds the Jewish people of their deliverance from Pharaoh |
| Paul | one of the apostles who was inspired by God to write portions of the New Testament |
| Pentecost | Feast of Harvest after Jesus had returned to heaven at which time the Holy Spirit came upon the believers in a special way |
| People of Israel | the People of the Old Testament covenant |
| Pharaoh | the ancient king of Egypt |
| Psalms | poems and hymns, many of which were written by David; also known as *Zabur* by Muslims |
| sacrifice | an offering often given as a sign of ones desire for forgiveness |
| salvation | the experience of forgiveness of sin and a right and joyous relationship with God |

| | |
|---|---|
| Satan | the devil |
| Saviour | Jesus means the Saviour, Who saves mankind from sin and evil |
| secular | pertaining to the earth in the present time |
| Sermon on the Mount | teachings on righteousness given by Jesus to His disciples |
| the shepherds | the people to whom the angels announced the birth of Jesus |
| Son of God | Messiah Who had a perfect relationship with God |
| the Spirit of God | sometimes also called the Holy Spirit. God is present among mankind as 'Spirit' |
| *Taurat* | See Torah |
| Ten Commandments | principles of right conduct which God revealed to the covenant people |
| testament | a solemn agreement or covenant |
| Torah | the first five books of the Bible, also called the Pentateuch of the Prophet Moses |
| Trinity | an attempt by Christians to express the unity and love of God as revealed in God as Creator, Saviour, and Spirit (Father, Son, Holy Spirit) |
| Virgin Mary | the mother of Jesus |
| wisemen | the men from the East who came to Jerusalem to find the Messiah at the time of His birth |
| Yahweh | the Hebrew name for God which was revealed to the Prophet Moses at the burning bush. This name means 'I AM' or 'I Will Be' or 'I Was'. It is God as the One Who enters into covenant with man |

# Select Bibliography

Ali, Abdullah Yusuf, *The Holy Qur'an: Text, Translation, and Commentary*, Delhi: Kutub Khana Isha'at-ul-Islam.

Anderson, J.N.D., *Christianity: The Witness of History*, London, Tyndale Press, 1970.

Anderson, W.B., *The Church in East Africa*, 1840–1974, Dodoma, Tanzania, Central Tanganyika Press, 1977.

Arberry, A.J., *The Koran Interpreted*, New York, Macmillan, 1955.

Azizullah, Muhammad, *Glimpses of the Hadith*, Takoma Park, Maryland, The Crescent Publications, 1973.

Brown, David, *The Christian Scriptures*, London, S.P.C.K.

—————, *The Church and the Churches*, London, S.P.C.K.

—————, *The Cross of the Messiah*, London, S.P.C.K.

—————, *The Divine Trinity*, London, S.P.C.K.

—————, *Jesus and God*, London, S.P.C.K.

Clark, Dennis E., *The Life and Teaching of Jesus the Messiah*, Elgin, Illinois, Dove Publications, 1977.

Cragg, Kenneth, *The Call of the Minaret*, New York, Oxford University Press, 1964.

—————, *The Dome and the Rock*, London, S.P.C.K. 1964.

—————, *The House of Islam*, Encino, California, Dickenson Publishing Co. Inc., 1975.

—————, and Speight, Marston, *Islam From Within: Anthology of a Religion*, Belmont, California, Wadsworth, 1980.

Dodd, C. H., *The Founder of Christianity*, New York, Macmillan, 1976.

Gibb, H.A.R., *Islam*, London, Oxford University Press.

Guillaume, Alfred, *Islam*, Penguin.

Hitti, Philip K., *History of the Arabs*, London, Macmillan, 1973.

*Holy Bible, The, New International Version*, Grand Rapids, Zondervan Bible Publishers, 1978.

*Holy Bible, The, Revised Standard Version*, Thomas Nelson & Sons.

*Islam: Our Choice*, Karachi: Begum Aisha Bawany Waqf, 1970.

*Islam the First and Final Religion*, Karachi, Begum Aisha Bawany Waqf, 1978.

Jomier, J., *Jesus, The Life of the Messiah*, Vaniyayambadi, India, Concordia, 1974.

Kealy, John P. and Shenk, David W., *The Early Church and Africa*, Nairobi, Oxford University Press, 1974.

King, Noel Q., *Christian and Muslim in Africa*, New York, Harper and Row, 1971.

Lewis, C. S., *Mere Christianity*, New York, Macmillan, 1960.

Maududi, S. Abul Ala, *Finality of Prophethood*, Nairobi, The Islamic Foundation, 1978.

——————, *Fundamentals of Islam*, Nairobi, The Islamic Foundation, 1976.

——————, *Islam: A Historical Perspective*, Leicester, England, The Islamic Foundation.

——————, *Islamic Way of Life*, Nairobi, The Islamic Foundation, 1978.

Miller, Donald G. *The Authority of the Bible*, Grand Rapids, Eerdmans, 1972.

Miller, William M., *Beliefs and Practices of the Christians*, Lahore, Masihi Isha'at Khana, 1975.

Newbigin, Lesslie, *The Open Secret*, Grand Rapids, Eerdmans, 1978.

Pickthall, Mohammed Marmaduke, *Holy Quran*, Karachi, Begum Aisha Bawany Waqf.

Qutb, Muhammad, *Islam the Misunderstood Religion*, Kuwait, Ministry of Awqaf and Islamic Affairs, 1964.

Rahman, Fazlur, *Islam*, New York, Holt, Rinehart and Winston, 1966.

Register, Ray G., *Dialogue and Interfaith Witness with Muslims*, Kingsport, Tennessee, Moody Books, Inc., 1979.

Saulat, Sarwat, *The Life of the Prophet*, Nairobi, Islamic Foundation, 1978.

Shari'at, Ali, *On the Sociology of Islam*, Berkeley, Mizan Press, 1979 (translated from Persian by Hamid Algar).

Shenk, David W., *The Holy Book of God: an Introduction*, Accra, A.C.P., 1980.

Trimingham, J. Spencer, *Islam in East Africa*, Oxford, Clarendon Press, 1964.

Watt, Montgomery W., *Mohammad, Prophet and Statesman*, London, Oxford University Press,